Published by
British Agencies for Adoption & Fostering
(BAAF)
Skyline House
200 Union Street
London SE1 OLX

Charity registration 275689

© BAAF 1984, 1986, 1990, 1995
Fifth edition 1998

© BAAF 1998

British Library Cataloguing in Publication Data
A catalogue reference record for this book is available from the
British Library

ISBN 1 873868 22 7

Illustrated by Sarah Rawlings
Designed by Andrew Haig & Associates
Typeset by Aldgate Press
Printed and bound by Stanley L. Hunt Ltd

Contents

About adoption

Finding an adoption agency

Acknowledgements

The first four editions of *Adopting A Child* were co-authored by Prue Chennells and Chris Hammond in 1984, 1986, 1990 and 1995.

This edition is closely based on the previous editions but contains new material and significant amendments in light of the Children Act 1989 and the Children (Scotland) Act 1995. Revisions and new material contained in this edition have been prepared by Jenifer Lord.

Our thanks go to the following people for all their suggestions and advice in the preparation of this edition including reading and commenting on the manuscript, rewriting sections or preparing new material, and preparing the text for production: Sheila Byrne, Susanne Clarke, Lizzi Gill, Jon Hawke, Greg Kelly, Jenifer Lord, Philly Morrall, Marjorie Morrison, Alexandra Plumtree, Shaila Shah, Marcia Spencer.

Introduction

About 6,300 children are adopted in the UK each year. We estimate that half of these are children adopted by their parent and step-parent. The others are mainly children looked after by local authorities, what used to be described as "in care", but they represent a tiny proportion, about five per cent, of all the children for whom local authorities are responsible. Most of the children looked after by local authorities return home to their own family quite quickly.

The majority of children who are adopted are aged five or more. There are single children and groups of brothers and sisters who need placement together and there are children with disabilities who range in age from babies upwards. There are children from a huge variety of ethnic, religious and cultural backgrounds, all of whom need families who match their backgrounds as closely as possible. Many of the children have been abused and/or neglected before they come into local authority care and they will have been further confused and upset by uncertainty and moves after coming into care.

Just as there is a wide range of children needing adoption, so will a wide range of people be welcomed by adoption agencies to adopt them. People of every ethnic, religious and cultural background, couples and single people – heterosexual as well as lesbian and gay – both with or without children, older people, people who have been divorced, all can and do become successful adoptive parents. And the great majority of adoptions work out well. Like all parents, adoptive parents get huge joy and satisfaction from parenting their children, as well as finding it very hard work and sometimes frustrating and painful.

Traditionally, adoption – for children not previously known to the families adopting them – was seen as severing connections with the past and starting afresh. Now we understand how important it is to provide adoptive parents with as much information as possible to pass on to their children, and how important their heritage is for those children. More and more of them, especially the older ones, are being adopted yet continue to maintain important relationships – sometimes with their birth parents, more often with other family members like brothers and sisters, grandparents, aunts and uncles.

Adoption agencies do not expect you to have all the answers before you approach them. They will provide information and opportunities for you to find out about what will be involved, for instance, by introducing you to experienced adoptive parents. They are also getting better at providing help and support to you and your child once you are living together and even after you have adopted. Help is also available from adoptive parents' support groups and from post-adoption centres.

We hope that this book will answer most of your initial questions as well as clarify anything that may have previously puzzled you about adoption – the processes, the cost, the legal issues, etc. All these and many other issues are addressed in this book. These are illustrated with real life experiences in which people candidly talk about what went right and what went wrong and how they were helped or helped themselves create a safe, secure and loving family environment for a child or children who needed this. Remember, for children who have to be separated from their birth families, having a new permanent family by adoption is very much a process and an experience that must fulfil *their* needs and help them through to a fulfilling adulthood.

A glossary of terms that are used in this book and which may be unfamiliar to you is provided at the end.

Note about this edition

In this edition, we have included some information about Northern Ireland. Although not comprehensive, we hope that most of the text will be of use to readers in Northern Ireland. However, it must be remembered that there are some differences in practice and procedures. For example, there are very few black children for adoption or in the care system in Northern Ireland. Also, there are still a number of babies who come into or are removed to care at a very early age and proceed to adoption once they have been "freed" for adoption. However, adoption as a route out of care for older children is not widely used although efforts are being made to develop this.

In Northern Ireland, personal social services are provided by 11 Health and Social Services Trusts in turn commissioned by four Health and Social Services Boards. Unlike England and Wales and Scotland, social services are not under local authority control although these arrangements could change in the near future. A list of all agencies appears later on in this book.

Lastly, throughout this text we have referred to local authority agencies or social services or social work departments. Although these terms are not accurate when applied to Northern Ireland for reasons explained above, we have used them for the sake of simplicity.

Children needing adoption

Sean and Simon are eight and nine and they've lived with us for two years. We adopted them nearly a year ago. We were totally exhausted for most of the first 18 months but we're starting to settle down now as a family and we have great fun together. The boys see their older sister, who's fostered, and also their grandmother, twice a year and that works well.

Probably at least 5,000 children currently in the care system in England, Scotland and Wales could be placed for adoption with families if the families were available. Although they are very different, they all have one thing in common: a need for a family.

It's recognised that, for nearly all children, life in a family is best. A new family can bring love and security to the child – and a child can bring joy and satisfaction to the family. Every child is different and brings the potential for different sorts of satisfaction just as they will bring their own set of needs and challenges. The agency's job – with your help – is to match that child's potential and needs with your abilities and expectations.

Are there any babies needing adoption?

Nowadays, adoption is rarely about babies because there are so few who need to be adopted. Around 6,300 children are adopted each year in the UK, although we estimate that about half are in-family adoptions of stepchildren. Fewer than 500 babies under one are adopted each year.

Times have changed. Today it is easier for women to choose to parent on their own and fewer single mothers are placing their babies for adoption. Contraception is also more efficient than it used to be, and fewer unplanned pregnancies occur. Also it is easier to get an abortion than previously.

There are many, many more white people interested in adopting a white baby without disabilities than there are such babies needing adoption. Agencies have no difficulty in finding suitable adopters for white babies without disabilities and many already have quite a few prospective adopters approved and waiting to adopt. This means that people who only want to adopt a child such as this are likely to find it hard even to get started on the adoption road and most will not be able to adopt a baby.

By contrast, agencies are less successful at finding black families or those from other minority ethnic groups, although they are getting better at it. This means that if you and/or your partner is black or from a minority ethnic group, you are likely to find an agency to take up your application quite quickly. You will probably have a shorter wait before being linked with a baby although this will vary as only quite small numbers of black babies and those from other minority ethnic groups are placed for adoption each year. If you can consider slightly older children, your wait could be shorter.

There are some babies with disabilities or disabling conditions such as Down's Syndrome and cerebral palsy who need to be adopted. There are also some babies with genetic factors in their background, such as schizophrenia or Huntington's Chorea, for whom it is not always easy to find adoptive families.

What about older children?

The majority of children waiting to be adopted are aged five or over. Older children can benefit from family life. They may have lived for some years with one or both of their parents, or they may have spent most of their lives in the care system. They may have had many moves in and out of children's homes and foster homes, and the damage done by these experiences can last a very long time. Older children need especially resilient parents who can help them face up to the past – including their need to keep in touch with some

Donna came to us when she was nine. She was so moody – lovely one day, terrible the next. We often wondered if we'd make it to adoption! We kept telling each other about the reasons she was so difficult – she'd had a hard life, moved from place to place. We still have some bad patches, but nothing like we used to. We wouldn't be without her for the world.

members of their family – and see them through the difficult adolescent years to maturity. In a loving and secure home, most of these children will eventually begin to thrive, although the older they are, the longer it may take.

Won't older children have a lot of problems?

Children who have been looked after by a local authority for months or years are likely to have emotional and behavioural problems because of the experiences which led to them having to be separated from their birth families, but also because of not having a permanent parent figure in their lives. Even young children soon learn there isn't much point in getting attached to an adult who is soon going to disappear out of their lives. They may find it difficult to become attached to a new family and may act up or test out the new parents in an effort to get the attention they have been missing. Young children may be more like babies in their behaviour sometimes, and even teenagers may act like very young children. But most children of all ages can eventually settle down when they realise that they really are part of the family.

I'm not married and I haven't any children of my own. When I discovered it was possible for single people to adopt, I went along to my local social work department and applied to take two school-age children. With three married brothers, all with children, I've had plenty of practice and I'm used to having children running around the house. The department took a bit of convincing but six months ago Vicky and her brother Tony joined me. Looking after two lively children of ten and eight is hard work and I'm glad that one of my brothers lives very close by. You do need help and support and someone to grumble at sometimes.

There are some children who have been so hurt by their experiences that they will go on having special needs throughout their childhood, even though they have clearly benefited from becoming a loved member of the family. If you choose to adopt a child who may have ongoing needs you should ensure that the agency will make arrangements for them to have any special help they may continue to require on a long-term basis.

Groups of brothers and sisters

Children from the same family often want to stay together, especially if they are older. Their brothers and sisters may be the only people in their lives who have stayed stable and reliable, and splitting them up might affect them badly. So families are needed for groups of brothers and sisters, two, three, four or even more. It may seem particularly difficult to take two or more children into a new family, but brothers and sisters can help and support each other.

Children with disabilities

Children with disabilities may be placed for adoption at a very young age when their parents feel unable to care for them, or they

> We've got three sons, and Danny, our youngest, was born with Down's Syndrome. When we saw the article in our local paper about four-year-old Annie needing a home it struck a chord at once; Annie's got Down's Syndrome too. Some people seemed to think it was odd that anyone would want a second child like that but we knew from experience how rewarding they can be – and we'd built up all that useful knowledge on schools and things for Danny already. Annie joined us nearly a year ago and we adopted her last month – the family wouldn't be the same without her.

may be looked after by the local authority after their parents have tried unsuccessfully to cope. So they may feel the impact both of their disability, the loss of their family of origin, and perhaps the confusion of a residential setting where different staff come and go. People who adopt these children will need to be prepared for a challenging yet rewarding task, as some of the children will never be able to lead entirely independent lives. In some cases, experience of disability in prospective adopters – either their own personal or professional experience or that of their children – will be positively welcomed. (See *Whatever happened to Adam?* in Further Reading.)

Learning disabilities/difficulties

There are many babies and older children who have learning difficulties/disabilities waiting for adoption. For example, children with Down's Syndrome. These are children who, as well as individual love and care, need additional help and support to enable them to participate in as many as possible of the experiences and opportunities open to any other child.

There are many children whose learning disabilities are not clear-cut: they may have suffered an accident or injury while very young which has affected their ability to learn or to understand the world around them – but no-one knows how much. Or they may have been born with a disability that isn't clear to doctors. Sometimes they may be physically disabled too. Just like any other children they all need love and attention and the opportunity of family life and they all respond to it.

Physical disabilities

There are many types of physical disability – cerebral palsy, muscular dystrophy, spina bifida and cystic fibrosis are just some of them. Children with these disabilities may need to wear calipers or to use wheelchairs all their lives but this doesn't mean that they don't need the love and security that life in a family offers. And, like most children, they will give love and affection in return. Having a physical disability does not mean having a learning disability too, although people sometimes confuse the two. People with physical disabilities can lead increasingly independent lives nowadays – especially if they have the support of a loving family.

Are both black and white children waiting to be adopted?

Yes, there are children from a great variety of ethnic, cultural and religious backgrounds waiting for adoption. They all need families who match their culture, "race", religion and language as closely as possible.

Do the children all have contact with their birth families? What is open adoption?

Open adoption is a term which means different things to different people. It can mean anything from an adoption where the child has regular face-to-face contact with members of his or her birth family to an adoption where the adopters have met the birth parents once and there is an annual letter exchanged via the adoption agency. Many children being placed for adoption now will have a plan for their adoptive parents to have an annual exchange of news with their birth family via the adoption agency. Others will need and want to meet members of their birth family, sometimes grandparents, brothers and sisters, as well as their parents, perhaps twice a year. You will need to be clear what the plan for contact is for any child whom you plan to adopt.

I'm from Jamaica and my husband is Scottish. We were shocked when we learnt how many children with one black and one white parent are in the care system. We've adopted Jamie, who is now four and we've just been matched with a little brother for him, who is two.

2

Who can adopt?

We can't have children of our own but we really wanted to be parents. After talking to a social worker in our local adoption agency we decided that we could consider school age children. Michael, aged eight and his sister, Hannah, aged seven were placed with us just a few months after we were approved.

Are there long waiting lists for adopters?

No! It is estimated that at least 5,000 children looked after by local authorities in England, Scotland and Wales could be adopted if enough adopters came forward. They are children like those described in the previous chapter and adopters, both couples and single people, those with or without children already and people of various ages are urgently needed to offer them a chance of family life. The only group of children for whom there are many more potential adopters than there are children, are white babies and toddlers without disabilities. Rather than keeping waiting lists of people wanting to adopt this group of children agencies usually have their lists closed. They then just recruit a few families as and when they need them for this small group of children.

Do I have to be "special" to adopt?

No, but understanding, energy, commitment, and the ability to face up to challenges and difficulties are all needed to care for an older child or a child with disabilities or a group of brothers and sisters. A good sense of humour helps too!

Just as you will be providing support and understanding to a child with a variety of different needs, so you will need support yourself. Your family, including your children if you have some, plus your close relatives and friends, need to be in agreement with your plan, because you will almost certainly call on them for help. Your immediate family will, like yourself, be very closely affected. Children who have been hurt by their experiences can easily hurt others in their search for security. You will need all the help you can get. In return, though, you will get all the joy and satisfaction of seeing some of the emotional damage to a child gradually start to heal.

Are there age limits?

You have to be at least 21 years old to adopt in law (unless you are a birth parent involved in a joint step-parent adoption, when the age is 18).

There is a greater health risk as people age. Agencies have a responsibility to ensure as far as possible that prospective adopters are likely to be fit and active at least until their child is a young adult. Some adult adopted people record their feelings of discomfort at being placed as young children with older adoptive parents. For these reasons many agencies would not normally expect there to be more than about a 40 to 45 year age gap between the child and their adoptive parents.

Birth mothers placing infants for adoption often ask for their child to be placed with parents within average childbearing ages. So, if agencies do, occasionally, take families on for babies for whom there is a huge choice of families, they may choose to work with slightly younger people.

Do I have to be married?

No. Single people, both men and women, can and do adopt. If you wish to adopt jointly with a partner the law requires you to be married. However, one partner in an unmarried couple – heterosexual or lesbian or gay – can adopt. The other partner could apply for a Residence Order. People who have been divorced can adopt. If you are married or in a partnership, adoption agencies usually prefer you to have been together for several years before taking up an adoption application from you.

Do I have to be British?

No. You are eligible to adopt a child in the UK if your permanent home is here (the legal term is "domicile"). In Scotland, you can also adopt if you have lived in the UK for more than one year, even if you do not have your permanent home here. In England and Wales, you are not eligible for a full Adoption Order unless you are domiciled in the UK. However, it is possible to obtain a court order authorising you to take a child from the UK to your home country to obtain a full Adoption Order there.

What if I'm British but working overseas for a few years?

Unless you are making arrangements for the adoption of a child already well known to you, you will not be able to adopt from the UK until you return to live here.

You need, for practical purposes, to be living in the UK for at least two years, so that the adoption agency has a chance to work with you and get to know you, and also to match you with a child and to introduce and place the child. This is followed by a period of at least three months, usually longer, before you can obtain an Adoption Order i.e. when parental responsibilities for the child are legally yours.

Most children needing adoption will already have had a number of moves. They are likely to be insecure and to need as much stability as possible. They may also have some ongoing contact with members of their birth family. For these reasons it may not be appropriate for many children to be placed with adopters who will be moving around a lot or living overseas after the child's adoption.

Doctors told us that there was no chance of us conceiving a second child. Our son, Mark, is now nine and very much wants a younger brother or even a sister! We saw David in *Be My Parent*. He's only six but he's already been excluded from school once. His local authority are assessing us just for him. We're excited although we know he'll be a challenge for us.

What if I have a disability or poor health?

Medical conditions or disability will not necessarily rule you out. All prospective adopters have to have a full medical examination done by their GP. The adoption agency employs a doctor who acts as a medical adviser. He or she may want your permission to contact consultants who have treated you. The adoption agency's prime concern is that you will have the health and vigour necessary to meet the needs of your child until he or she is a young adult.

There is evidence that smoking causes health problems for smokers and that passive smoking can damage the health of others, particularly young children. For this reason, many agencies will not usually place pre-school children with people who smoke.

Excessive alcohol consumption also leads to health problems. It may also be associated, for children in care, with violence and physical abuse. Your drinking habits will therefore need to be discussed with you.

There is also evidence that obesity can cause health problems as can anorexia or other eating disorders and so these conditions are carefully considered by the agency.

What if I've got a criminal record?

People with a record of offences against children or who are known to have harmed children are not considered by adoption agencies. A criminal record of other offences need not rule you out. However, the nature of the offence and how long ago it was committed will have to be carefully considered. It is important to be open and honest with the adoption agency early on if you have a criminal record. The information will come to light when the police and other checks are done and any attempt at deception by you will be taken very seriously.

What about finances and housing?

You do not have to own your own home or to be wealthy. You may be eligible to receive an Adoption Allowance from the local authority in certain circumstances such as if the child whom you wish to adopt has special needs and if you could not afford to adopt him or her otherwise.

Does it matter if we're still having treatment for infertility?

Yes. It is not a good idea to be actively trying to conceive a child at the same time as considering adoption. Adoption agencies will want you to have ceased infertility treatment before contacting them.

We'd like to adopt a child the same age as our son so that they can grow up together

There is quite a lot of research evidence which shows that it is much more likely that things will not work if a child joining a family is close in age to a child already there. Agencies, therefore, usually prefer to have an age difference of two years or more between children. It is also often easier for the new child if he or she can join your family as the youngest child. However, it is possible for children to come in as the eldest or as a middle child, so do discuss this with the adoption agency if you feel it might work in your family.

> We really wanted to adopt a young child, but we knew we'd have to be flexible. Our son, Alex, was only five months old when he came to us. His mother suffers from schizophrenia and his father may do as well and so we've accepted that Alex is more at risk than most people of developing a mental illness when he's older. We'll help and support him all we can should he become ill.

I'm white and I'd like to be considered for black children as well as white children

The Guidance to the Children Act 1989 for England and Wales states that 'it may be taken as a guiding principle of good practice that, other things being equal and in the great majority of cases, placement with a family of similar ethnic origin and religion is most likely to meet a child's needs as fully as possible and to safeguard his or her welfare most effectively'. Scottish legislation is similar.

There are more white children than black children needing adoption and so it makes much more sense for white families to adopt white children whose needs they can meet as fully as possible. For instance, agencies would aim to place a child from an Irish Catholic background with Irish Catholic adopters rather than with an English family who are Baptists.

However much we may dislike it, we have to accept the fact that racism is still common in Britain today. So black children – including those of mixed (black and white) parentage who will be identified as black – will, sooner or later, have to cope with some form of racism. A black child who faces racist abuse outside the home will find it easier to discuss what has happened, understand it, and learn how to deal with it from a black adopter who can immediately relate to this experience. Coping with racism is something white people are not geared to, whereas for black adults it is a fact of life. Black children need this level of support in their daily life.

Black children also need black adults they can look up to. Images of black people on television, radio and in newspapers are often negative although this is slowly changing. Black children need to see black adults presented in a positive way so that they can respect them and grow up like them. For children who have been unable to stay with their own black families and who are then placed in white families, it can be hard to correct the false impression that white is better than black.

For black children and those from other minority ethnic groups, maintaining links with family members is important just as it would be for a white child. Matching heritage between a child and the adoptive family will make it easier for the child to settle, will help facilitate any continuing birth family contact, and will have the long-term advantage of the child learning about his or her heritage and culture.

In those instances where white families do adopt black children, they will need to encourage their children to be part of their own black community. They need to prepare them for the problems they will face and explain to them that although their parents detest racism, it still has to be faced in the world outside. This subject is tackled in greater detail in the companion book *Talking about adoption to your adopted child* (see Useful Reading).

I'm worried about an open adoption. Will this rule me out?

It depends what you mean by an open adoption. The term is used to mean anything from a one-off meeting with your child's birth parents and an annual exchange of news via the adoption agency to regular face-to-face contact between your child and members of their birth family. It is recognised now that it can be helpful for some children to maintain some face-to-face contact, perhaps with a grandparent or a brother or sister and sometimes with their birth parents. Face-to-face contact is not the plan for all children and you can discuss with the agency your wish not to have a child who needs this to be linked with you.

However, *all* adoptive parents need to have an open attitude to their child's birth family and past. You need to recognise the importance of this for your child and be prepared to talk with your child about his or her often confused feelings about their birth family and their past. You also have to accept that things can change and that your child *may* want direct contact in the future even though that isn't the plan now.

A one-off meeting with birth parents can be very valuable in helping you talk with your child about their birth family and it can be reassuring for the child to know that you have met his or her birth parents. Most adoption agencies would expect you to be prepared for a one-off meeting. They would also expect that you could consider at least an annual exchange of news, usually anonymously via the adoption agency, with your child's birth parents.

How do I go about adopting a child?

We were a bit overwhelmed by all the children in *Be My Parent*. However, the social worker from our local adoption agency was really helpful and we're now hoping to be approved for two children aged between four and eight.

First steps

It can be helpful to do a bit of reading about adoption as it is today and about the sorts of children needing families before you approach an adoption agency. This book is a good start and other useful books and leaflets are listed at the end.

Many people thinking about adoption also often find it invaluable to speak to experienced adopters. PPIAS is a self-help group for adoptive and prospective adoptive parents. It has local groups throughout the country whose members will be pleased to talk to you (see Useful Organisations).

Contacting an agency

This important step is fully covered in Chapter 8, followed by a complete list of adoption agencies in England, Wales, Scotland and Northern Ireland.

Can I respond to children I see advertised before I contact a local agency?

Yes, you can. Social workers featuring children in *Be My Parent*, *Adoption UK*, local newspapers and other media are happy to hear from unapproved families. However, their priority is to place their child with a suitable family as soon as possible and so they will follow up approved families first. However, if you are within their geographical catchment area they may well decide to take up an application from you. This might be because you are the most suitable (or the only!) family who has responded to their child. It might also be because they think that you are offering a valuable resource to a child, even if they cannot place the child to whom you have responded with you.

The child's social worker might ask an agency local to you to do the assessment on their behalf, if you live at a distance. Alternatively, he or she might suggest that you contact a local agency, as there are other possibilities for the child whom they have featured.

As discussed in Chapter 8, you need to think carefully about being assessed by an agency a long way away as it may be difficult for them to offer you adequate help and support once you have a child placed with you.

What is the assessment or home study?

This is the process by which the adoption agency gets to know you and assesses your ability to parent an adopted child. It is also the process by which you learn about what will be involved in this parenting task and consider, in partnership with the social workers, whether you have the necessary skills and strengths. You will need to be open and honest with the social workers – they will get suspicious if they think you are too perfect! They need to know what your limitations are (everyone has some) so that they can make sure that suitable help and support are provided.

What exactly are they looking for?

Social workers are looking for people who are open and honest about their limitations as well as their strengths; people who are adaptable and flexible and willing to learn; people who enjoy children and are willing and able to put the child's needs first; people who know that every child, even a tiny baby, comes with a past and a birth family who are important; and people with "staying power" and a sense of humour.

What exactly will happen and how long will it take?

Each agency works in a slightly different way. However, most will ask you to attend a series of group meetings, where you can meet other prospective adopters and can learn with them something of what adoption and being an adoptive parent is all about. Adult adopted people, experienced adopters and birth parents whose children have been adopted often speak at these groups. There will also be individual interviews with you as well as joint interviews with your partner if you have one. Your own children, if you have any, will be fully involved.

You will have to have a medical examination done by your GP. Checks will be carried out with the police and other agencies and two personal referees will be interviewed. Obviously this will all be discussed with you first and your written permission will be needed for these checks to be made.

A written report will be compiled, usually with your help. BAAF's Form F1 is the form most often used to collate this information. You should certainly see the report, apart from the medical information and checks, and you should comment, in writing if necessary, on anything that you disagree with the social worker about or that you think should be added.

The report is then presented to the agency's adoption panel for their recommendation. This is a group of people, including social work professionals, medical and legal advisers, councillors and others with an interest in adoption. It usually includes at least one adoptive parent. The rules about panels are different in England and Wales from Scotland, but the idea is the same: to consider prospective adopters and make a recommendation to the agency about whether they are approved or not.

In Scotland, prospective adopters must be invited to the panel, and many agencies elsewhere do invite prospective adopters too. You could ask whether the agency you plan to work with offers this.

After the panel has made its recommendation, a senior officer in the agency makes a decision about whether or not to approve you as an adopter. In England and Wales, if the agency is proposing not to approve you, they must write to you first giving you their reasons and asking for your comments. In England, Wales and Scotland, the agency must write and tell you their decision, whether it is approval or non-approval. It should be unlikely for you to get to this stage and not be aware of any concerns about you from your social worker.

This process, from work starting to approval by the agency usually takes between four to six months. It is described more fully in BAAF's leaflet, *Understanding the Assessment Process* (see Useful Reading).

What happens after approval?

If you have been approved by a local authority, they will consider you carefully for their waiting children. They will usually want you to wait for one of their children for several months before responding to children advertised by other agencies. You may want to check on this before deciding to work with them.

If you have been approved by a voluntary adoption agency, they will help you to find a waiting child. They will encourage you to respond to children in *Be My Parent*, *Adoption UK* and other media. You should also discuss with them referrals to BAAF*Link*, BAAF's computer linking service.

There may also be more local linking services available to you. For example, in Scotland, BAAF runs the Scottish Resource Network which has a newsletter of Scottish children waiting. In addition there is the more local West of Scotland Consortium. A number of local consortia are also operating in various parts of England. Your agency should be able to tell you about them.

What happens if I'm not approved?

If the agency has not been able to approve you, you should discuss with them fully the reasons why. They will have been disappointed not to be able to approve you and will have thought about this very carefully and so you may agree with them that perhaps adoption is not for you. However, you can, if you wish, approach other adoption agencies and start again. Sometimes, people turned down by one agency are approved by another and go on to adopt successfully.

If you feel that the service that you have had from the agency has been very poor you can, if you wish, make a formal complaint about this to the agency.

| How am I matched with a child?

Your agency may approach you to discuss a possible child or you may respond to a child whom you see featured as needing a new family. You will probably talk with your own social worker first and will then meet the child's social worker and also, perhaps, their foster carer. You will also be given written information about the child. It is important, in the excitement of hearing about a possible child at last, that you take time to consider the child's needs carefully. You may want to follow up particular issues with the social workers or the foster carers or with a doctor, or check whether the necessary services, eg. special schooling, are available in your area.

However, if everyone decides that you really do seem to be right for a particular child, the match will be taken to an adoption panel, usually the one in the child's local authority. Your Form F1, the child's Form E (a lengthy report, comparable to your Form F and which you should have read) and a report stating why you seem to be right for the child, will be presented to the panel. Your social worker and the child's social worker will attend. As with your approval as an adopter, it is a senior officer who makes the decision about the match, based on the recommendation of the panel.

| How long will it be before my
| child comes to live with me?

Once a decision has been made about a match, the social workers will work out with you a plan for introducing you and the child to each other. Introductions may be daily for a week for a baby, or rather more spaced out over a longer period for an older child. They do not usually last more than six to eight weeks though.

You should discuss any doubts or concerns that you may have with the social workers during this period. If you really do not feel that the match is right it is much better to say so at this stage rather than later.

4

What about adoption from abroad?

I know that there are older children needing adoption here, but I really, really wanted to adopt a baby. I had a home study done by my local social services department and then I managed to find my baby daughter through a welfare agency in Guatemala. I'm lucky that my cousin is married to a Guatemalan man and he's going to be very important to my daughter as she grows up.

Many families want or only feel able to parent a young child without special needs and it is these families, among others, who often decide to try and adopt from overseas.

Where can I get advice and help before deciding on this?

You can approach your local social services or social work department. They will be pleased to have an opportunity to meet and talk with you before you make an application to adopt from overseas. There is also a helpline run by the Department of Health and another run independently by the Overseas Adoption Helpline. PPIAS (Parent to Parent Information on Adoption Services) will be able to talk to you about adoption generally and AFAA (Association of Families who have Adopted from Abroad) will be able to help you with some of the issues particular to adoption from overseas. Written information is available from all these agencies and from BAAF. (See Useful Organisations and Useful Books.) Many of the issues that you will need to consider are also relevant for adoption in the UK and are covered in Chapter 2.

Surely adoption overseas is the best plan for children living in large institutions?

It may be the best plan for some children in the short term. However, children have the right to remain in their own family, their own community and their own country if at all possible and countries overseas are working to this end. They need help from more affluent countries, and from individuals in those countries, to achieve this. The bureaucracy involved in intercountry adoption can be a distraction from this, diverting much needed resources.

> **We adopted two children from El Salvador. Our son isn't interested in his birth family, but our daughter is sad and angry that we have virtually no information about her first family. She blames us for this.**

As children grow up they may feel a deep anger and sadness and sense of loss at having been "rejected" not just by their birth family, but by their country of birth. It will be extremely difficult for them to establish any links with their birth family and with their past unless their adoptive parents have made great efforts to keep this alive for them.

If the child has been placed with adoptive parents of a different culture, "race", religion and language they will also be disadvantaged in establishing a positive sense of identity, and in coping with the racism which they will encounter.

Wouldn't countries in crisis welcome this sort of help?

It is dangerous to assume that in a situation of crisis, an easy answer is to adopt a child out of that country. In an emergency, it is impossible to gather the information needed to make a decision about whether the child really needs adoption. For example, are the child's parents alive or not? They may be in hospital, in prison or in hiding – and may re-emerge to claim their child later. Intercountry adoption is not a suitable way of dealing with the needs of children who are moved as a result of war, famine, or other emergency. Indeed, many of these children will be emotionally damaged by abandonment, malnutrition, the effects of war, and separation from their families. In a crisis, the child needs to be made safe in as familiar an environment as possible. Experienced aid workers find that the vast majority of children separated from their families by war or other emergency can be reunited with parents when the crisis recedes. What is required is temporary care in a secure and loving environment, not the permanence of adoption.

I really only want a child without health problems

There can be no guarantee about this when you adopt from overseas. There is often very little information available about the child's birth parents and so there may be unknown genetic factors, eg. schizophrenia, which will have implications for the child. The child may have been exposed to the risk of conditions such as tuberculosis, HIV infection, Hepatitis B and C. Reliable and safe testing may not be available. The child may also have suffered considerable emotional and intellectual deprivation which may have long-term effects.

Do I have to have a home study done?

Yes. You must have a home study done by the social services or social work department for the area where you live or by an approved voluntary adoption agency which is also approved as an intercountry adoption agency. The home study report is sent to the Department of Health or the Scottish Office and it is they who issue a Certificate of Approval. Some of the issues which will be covered in the home study are discussed in Chapter 3.

Is the whole process expensive?

Yes, it certainly can be. Most local authorities in the UK, whose first priority must be the children whom they are already looking after, make a charge for the home study to cover their costs. Charges range from about £700 to £3,000 or more. There will also be the cost of travel at least once, or possibly more often, to the child's country. Documents need to be translated and there are lawyer's fees.

Our daughter has a serious congenital hearing loss which we didn't know about when we adopted her from China. We love her and we are coping, although we'd always said that we didn't want to adopt a child with a disability.

How do I decide which country to apply to?

The home study must be in relation to one country only and it is for you to decide which one. It should be a country with which you already have links or can make links. It will be important for your child for you to have knowledge and understanding of the culture, religion and history of the country and, if possible and realistic, some knowledge of the language. You will need to know, or be prepared to get to know, adults from the country who are willing to play a part in your child's life.

How will I be linked with a child?

Once the Department of Health or the Scottish Office has issued a Certificate of Approval it will send all your papers to an agency in the country you have chosen. A child within the range for which you have been approved will then be identified. You will then have to travel to the child's country to meet the child. After obtaining entry clearance to the UK for the child, and completing formalities in the child's own country, you can return to the UK with your child.

Will I have to adopt the child again in the UK?

Yes, unless you adopt from a "designated" country whose adoption orders are recognised by the UK. You can get a list of these countries from the Department of Health or the Scottish Office.

What support will be available after I adopt?

The adoption agency which does your home study should discuss with you what support they can offer after adoption. There are post-adoption centres which can help you and there are also two support groups of adoptive parents, PPIAS and AFAA (see Useful Organisations).

How is adoption made legal?

We seemed to wait ages for the day of the adoption hearing to come round – in the end it only seemed to take a few minutes! We all went home and celebrated – it was such an important day for us and for Darren.

When you adopt a child, you become the child's legal parent. The child usually takes your surname and will inherit from you just as if he or she was born to you. All responsibility for making decisions about the child and his or her future is transferred to the adopters.

Adoption does not just happen automatically – you have to apply to court for an Adoption Order. You can go to your local Magistrates' Court, to the County Court, or to the High Court; in Scotland to the Sheriff Court or the Court of Session; in Northern Ireland to the County Court or to the High Court. The adoption agency should be able to help you with the process and the court. They will tell you what to do and the court will let you know when your case is going to be heard. An adoption is not legal without an Adoption Order.

How long does it take?

You can apply for an Adoption Order as soon as the child comes to live with you, but your application cannot be granted in court until the child has lived with you for at least three months. If your child has special needs, you will probably want to wait longer and give yourselves a chance to settle down together properly before applying to court. You will need to discuss with your social worker when the right time would be to apply to court. If a baby comes to you soon after birth, the order cannot be granted until the child is at least 19 weeks old. If you adopt a child from overseas, the period the child must live with you before an order can be made is 12 months.

What happens in court?

Adoption hearings are usually very short if the child's birth parents are in agreement, and in Scotland you may not need to go to court. You need not expect it to last more than half an hour, and you should be told at once whether the Adoption Order is granted. A report will have been prepared for the court which the judge, magistrates or sheriff will consider. You will probably be asked some questions, and so will the child, if he or she is old enough. The judge must consider the views of the child taking account of the child's age, understanding, etc. Also, in Scotland, any child of 12 or over is asked formally if he or she consents to the adoption. If there is no consent, the only reason to dispense or do away with that is if the child is incapable of consenting.

What if the birth parents don't agree?

If the birth parents do not agree, the adopters have to ask the court to over-ride their wishes, which it can only do in appropriate circumstances, for instance, if the parents are unreasonably refusing to agree. Cases like this are known as "contested adoptions" and if you are involved in one you will almost certainly need legal help. You may be able to obtain help with the costs, either through legal aid or from the adoption agency, and it is worth finding out about this at an early stage.

Can't the adoption agency sort this out earlier?

Adoption agencies sometimes go to court for a "freeing order" for a child, either because the birth parents want to agree to adoption early, or because the agency wants to look for a family for the child against the parents' wishes. Once the child has been "freed", the birth parents cannot stop an adoption going through.

Are there any other legal issues?

Yes, a few, but if, as is likely, you are adopting through an adoption agency, it will usually sort things out for you. You can only receive a child for adoption in this country if he or she is placed by a British adoption agency, unless the child is a close relative. Remember that any other private arrangement to adopt is illegal. Also, two people can only apply to adopt a child *jointly* if they are married. If you are not married, only one of you can apply to adopt and be named in the Adoption Order. The other partner could apply for a Residence Order.

Will my child get a new birth certificate when he is adopted?

Yes, your child will be issued with a new short certificate in your name which is the same as other short birth certificates. If you wish, you can apply for a long "birth" certificate, which will give your names and your child's new name. It will have "Copy of an entry in the adoption register" printed on it.

Is financial help available?

Adoption itself does not usually cost very much unless it is contested – it is afterwards that it gets expensive! If you're interested in adopting a child, but concerned about finances, you should talk to your adoption agency about adoption allowances. In some cases adoptive parents can get extra financial help if the child has particular needs which would make it hard for him or her to be adopted without such help. This must usually be discussed with the social worker before placement, and should normally be decided well before the adoption goes through. Adoption allowances are means tested. It is also possible for adopters to get a "settling in" grant, to help towards the cost of, for instance, beds or other equipment. This may be needed particularly when a group of brothers and sisters is being placed.

Do I have to pay the agency?

There is no charge for the home study, assessment and preparation if you are adopting a child who is in the UK. However, if you are asking an agency to do a home study so you can adopt a child from abroad, they will probably make a charge (see Chapter 4).

Our boys were ten and eight when they came to live with us. We couldn't manage without an adoption allowance, which is paid by the local authority that had our children in care.

What about medical examinations?

Adoption agencies have to make sure that adopters are healthy enough to take on the care of a child and are likely to live long enough to look after him or her until adulthood. The agency will provide a form for this: your GP examines you and fills it in. In most cases, you will have to pay the doctor's fee although sometimes the adoption agency can pay this. In Scotland, the cost is met by the Health Board.

Your adopted child needs a medical examination too, but this is the responsibility of the agency looking after the child.

Isn't going to court expensive?

There is a court fee which is currently £100 in the County Court or £30 in the Magistrates Court in England and Wales. In Scotland the fee at the Sheriff court is £45. The local authority responsible for the child may be able to help you with part or all of this fee.

What about legal fees?

If the birth parents do not agree to the adoption and decide to oppose it in court, it may get so complicated that you need a solicitor and a barrister, or in Scotland, an advocate. This means legal costs can rise, in some cases, to several thousand pounds. But you may be able to claim legal aid – it depends on your income – or the local authority responsible for the child will usually pay most, or all, of the legal costs involved.

What about costs after the adoption has gone through?

Unless an Adoption Allowance has been agreed when the child is legally yours the financial responsibility is also yours – just as it would be if you had given birth to the child yourself.

What happens after adoption?

We'd been to all the groups, talked to other people who'd adopted – we thought we could handle anything Andrew might do when he came to live with us. We just didn't expect him to do nothing! Not talk to us, not join in anything we did – it was a real effort for him just to sit and eat with us. He even packed a case and walked out on one occasion. We had (and needed!) a huge amount of help and support from our social worker and from our local adopters' support group. Andrew had a lot of help too and gradually he started to relax and to begin to trust us. We still have our ups and downs and family life isn't quite what we expected, but we are a family now.

Adoption is only the beginning. Adjusting to a different way of life will take time and there will be difficult periods. You may want to talk things over and get further advice and support either from the original adoption agency or from one of the specialist post-adoption projects which exist in many parts of the country.

What about the birth family?

Birth parents whose children are adopted usually find this a hard and painful experience. Sometimes they have requested adoption, but often the decision has been made by others, sometimes very much against their own wishes. However, they are often still very important to their children and many of them are prepared to co-operate with the adopters and the agency in offering what they can to their child.

It is usually to the benefit of the child if the adopters can meet the birth parents at least once and continue to exchange basic information about the child. This is usually through the adoption agency which acts as a "post box" for a letter perhaps once a year. It is now recognised that maintaining some level of contact can be of benefit to children as they grow up and helps the adopters answer questions about the birth parents, what they were like, where they are now, and so on. Obviously ongoing contact will not be right in all cases and will need to be handled sensitively.

This is something you and your agency will be discussing right from the start, so that when you become an adoptive parent you will have a clear idea of what sort of contact is likely to be the most helpful for your child. When agencies talk about contact they do not necessarily mean face-to-face meetings – in fact many arrangements for contact involve keeping in touch through letters and, perhaps, phone calls and are often through an intermediary such as the agency. Only some contact arrangements, at present, involve regular meetings between the child and people from his or her past.

For older children visits may continue after adoption. Brothers and sisters may be in touch, or perhaps birth parents, grandparents and other significant adults. Older children may well know where their relatives are living and want a family who can help them keep in contact. Again, this is something that you, the agency, and the child, if old enough, will need to discuss and agree on well before the adoption goes through to court.

Why do children have to know they are adopted?

The majority of children who are adopted are aged five or more and so they obviously know about their adoption. However, all children have the right to know about their past. Increasingly, it has been acknowledged that an open rather than a secretive attitude is more helpful to the child. After all, there is always the danger that someone else will tell the child without any warning, or perhaps in a hostile way, for example, in a family row. Finding out like this can be a terrible shock to a child who may well wonder what else you have concealed from them.

Even older children may be very confused about what happened in the past. They may blame themselves for the things that went wrong in their birth family. So it is important to be honest and to discuss adoption quite naturally, right from the start.

> I was really upset at first when Petra said she wanted to find out more about her "real" mother. Somehow it felt as if she must be unhappy with us. She always knew she was adopted and we'd told her what we knew about her mother, but she said she wanted some of the gaps filled in. Anyway, I helped her to get in touch with the adoption agency in the end, and having all the extra information really seemed to help. In fact, it's brought us closer together talking it all through.

From the age of 18 – 16 in Scotland – adopted children have the right to their original birth certificate if they want it – although their adoptive parents may already have given it to them.

Adoption means that the new parents must be prepared to be open with their child. Our book, *Talking about adoption to your adopted child*, can help you with the kind of issues you will face (see Useful Reading). This is when the information collected by the adoption agency about the child's parents, often in a life story book, will be needed. Children who are not given any facts sometimes have fantasies about their circumstances or history and may well believe the worst, so it is kinder and fairer to tell them the truth. This is not something that you do just once. Children need to go over their story again at different stages in their growing up, understanding a bit more each time.

What help will be available after adoption?

Social workers from the adoption agency you dealt with will offer you all the help they can during the settling-in period, and afterwards. Your local social services or social work department should be able to offer help too, after adoption, if you approach them. Specialist post-adoption centres have much experience in offering help and advice too. The Parent to Parent Information on Adoption Service (PPIAS) offers invaluable support and help to adoptive families. There are local groups throughout the country. The National Organisation for Counselling Adoptees and Parents (NORCAP) also offers support to adopted adults and their families. In Scotland, local authority adoption agencies now have to provide help for children who have been adopted, adoptive families, and others in their area. All these are listed in Useful Organisations.

It is useful to ask your social worker about sources of professional help or appropriate therapies. This will be especially important if you are adopting an older child who may have experienced considerable trauma, or a child who has suffered from neglect or abuse. In such cases, access to appropriate help will be crucial.

What if adoption goes wrong?

Some adoptions do go wrong – like marriages, they do not always work. The first few weeks and months can produce problems that no-one anticipated so there is always a settling-in period of at least three months. Of course, the social worker from the agency will keep in touch with you and will help and support you as much as possible. If you feel that things really are going wrong during this period and that you cannot continue with the child, you owe it to yourself and to the child to tell the agency.

Once the adoption has been made legal, the child will be legally yours just as if you had given birth to him or her. The sources of help described above will be available. However, if the problems cannot be resolved the social services or social work department can take responsibility for the child.

What will happen to the child if things don't work out?

If the child does have to leave, he or she will go either to a foster family or possibly to a residential home. If it isn't possible to resolve the difficulties with you, another adoptive home may be found – but the difficulties that arose between you and the child will have to be understood to try and prevent the same thing happening again. Sometimes agencies arrange a meeting – called a disruption meeting – which enables everyone concerned to come together and reflect on events and what can be learned from them. Sometimes the problems arise when the child is much older – 16 plus – and like many teenagers, is having difficulty feeling at home in a family setting. The best solution then may be to support the child in an "independent" setting such as lodgings. He or she may well value having you around to advise and reassure him or her even if living together is too difficult at that point in their lives.

Could I try again?

You may feel you and the child were not right for one another, and that you could succeed with a different child. If the social worker agrees with you, you may get the chance to adopt again. After all, different children need different families and just as a second attempt may work for a child, so it may work for a family. You could apply to the same agency again or to a different one. You would need a further period of assessment and preparation and the adoption panel and the agency would need to consider whether or not to approve you again to adopt.

What about fostering?

We've decided to apply for a Residence
Order on Gareth. We've fostered him
ever since he was nine – he's 13 now –
and although he still sees his mother
every month, there's no chance of them
living together again, at least not till
he's grown up. We'd like to be able to
make more decisions about him. Gareth
and his mum and his social worker
agree. Gareth's part of our family now
and that's all there is to it.

Fostering is a way of providing family life for someone else's child in your home. Most of the children looked after by local authorities when their own families are unable to care for them are placed in foster families. There are roughly 33,000 children in foster care in England and Wales, a figure which has remained relatively stable over the last 30 years, even though the total number of looked after children has fallen considerably in recent years. Families are unable to care for their children for a variety of reasons. Sometimes parents have poor physical or mental health and have to be hospitalised, or they may abuse drugs or alcohol and need help to overcome their addiction. Children may have been neglected and they may also have been abused.

What about the foster child's parents?

Fostering is shared caring. Foster carers are not the child's legal parents; they usually share the caring with the child's birth parents. Being a parent whose child is in foster care is painful, and foster carers need to understand this and to be sympathetic. Although they are not living with them, their parents are still very important to children who are fostered. Usually, they will want to see them often and parents will have a big part to play in making plans for the children's future, so foster carers and parents generally work closely together to do what is best for the children.

> We sort of became foster parents by accident – one of the neighbours was rushed to hospital and we looked after the two little girls until she was better. It made us think – we'd enjoyed having them, maybe we could help other mums and dads in the same way. Since then, we've fostered nearly 50 children. Most of them have gone home again pretty quickly, but one or two have had to stay longer. Some of them have kept in touch – one of our first foster kids brought his wife and baby to see us the other day.

Children in foster care are usually visited by their parents in the foster home and visit them in return. Foster carers must be prepared to help make these visits as easy as possible, in spite of all the uncertainties. And sometimes part of the task is helping the parent learn to care for the child. Other relatives, like brothers or sisters or grandparents, may also keep in touch with the child, and foster carers need to encourage this.

Are there different kinds of fostering?

Yes. Some parents make private arrangements for their children to be looked after by foster carers. There are special regulations for private fostering (see Useful Reading). The majority of foster children are looked after by local authorities. These agencies work with parents to make plans for the children. Their parents may have asked for them to be looked after, or a court may have ordered that a local authority should share responsibility with their parents. In Scotland, a Children's Hearing may have made a supervision requirement, with a condition that the children reside with foster carers. Also, in Scotland, the court may have granted a Parental Responsibilities Order to the local authority giving them almost all parental responsibilities and rights and the local authority may have the child looked after by foster carers.

There are a number of specialist fostering schemes which your local authority or a neighbouring one may run. For example, some children need very temporary care, but on a regular basis, perhaps one or two weekends a month. This is often called respite care. Other children and young people need family care following a court appearance and this is often called remand fostering.

Could I foster a baby?

You can say which age children you would prefer to foster and, if you prefer to look after babies or small children, you should say so. But it is important to remember that fostering is not a way into adopting a baby or young child. You will be expected to care for the child short-term until he or she returns home or until other plans are made.

Fostering isn't adoption

The vast majority of fostered children are able to return to their birth families. Many children need help for only a few days or weeks, but others may stay for months or even several years while attempts are made to resolve the family's problems. For a small number of children, adoption becomes the plan and foster carers have an important role in helping the child to move on to their new permanent family.

Fostering is not a back door to adoption and should not be viewed as such. You have to get used to seeing a child leaving your home, a child you have grown to love. But it can be very satisfying – children who arrive frightened and upset can leave feeling much more confident. Helping a child move on is one of the most important tasks of foster carers.

Occasionally, there might be agreement between social services and yourself that it would be best for a particular child to remain with you or be adopted by you. This would need full and careful discussion and you would need to be re-assessed and approved as an adoptive parent.

If you have fostered a child for some time and you want to adopt, it is possible to apply to court for an Adoption Order, but you may not be successful. The law treats the child's interests as the most important factor.

What about long-term fostering?

Sometimes, particularly for children aged 10 or over, foster care may be the plan until the child grows up. This long-term fostering cannot provide the same legal security as adoption for either the child or the foster family, but it may be the right plan for some children.

Some older children may accept, reluctantly, that they will never be able to return home to live and that they need a new family. However, they may be clear that they do not want to be adopted. They may also need a lot of extra help, for example, special schooling, hospital appointments, regular therapy sessions. You may decide that you would like to work in partnership with the local authority to offer long-term fostering to a child or young person. The child would remain the legal responsibility of the local authority and of their birth parents. You would receive a regular fostering allowance as well as being able to call on the local authority for help and support. You need to understand that most of the children for whom long-term fostering is the plan are at least nine or 10 years old.

What kind of people become foster carers?

Many different kinds of people are able to give children a loving and secure foster home. Some foster carers have young children of their own; some are older people whose children are now adults; others may not have any children of their own. Some people foster one child at a time, others more than one; some foster only babies or toddlers, others particularly like to look after teenagers. Foster carers come from all walks of life and live in all kinds of homes. It is the job of the social worker in the local authority or child care agency to find the right foster carers for each child, and this includes considering cultural and religious factors, among others.

> **I was a teacher of children with emotional difficulties and I first started fostering informally, caring for a couple of the children over the weekends during school holidays. Over the years I've cut down on the teaching and become a regular foster carer for my local authority. They tend to send me the older children with behaviour problems. I think they feel that I have the right background for it!**

Would I get paid?

Parents may make their own arrangements about payment for private fostering, but when children are looked after by local authorities foster carers are paid an allowance. This allowance covers the cost of feeding, clothing and looking after the child. Fostering allowances vary from area to area and according to the age and needs of the child.

Sometimes, foster carers are paid more than just their allowances for looking after a child. They can be paid a fee for looking after a child who needs special care. For example, a child with a physical or learning disability may need round-the-clock care and many visits to hospital.

How would I go about fostering a child?

First of all, you need to contact your local authority. If you look up the name of your council or a neighbouring one in the phone book, the social services (England and Wales) or social work department (Scotland) or Health and Social Services Board (Northern Ireland) should be listed; ask for the Fostering Officer. Social workers in local authorities often recruit foster carers through publicity in posters, leaflets and newspapers.

As a foster carer, you have to work closely with the child's social worker as well as with the child's birth family. In the early stages this will ensure that you know everything possible about the child, his or her likes and dislikes, normal routine, favourite foods and toys, etc. Later you would need to discuss the child's progress regularly with the worker and help plan for his or her future.

We've fostered Stephen since he was 11. He still has regular contact with his birth family and he has never wanted to be adopted. We feel we're giving him a good start into independent adult living. We'll always be there for him, just as his birth family are.

| Would I get training?

Many agencies run preparation and training groups for prospective foster carers as well as meeting with you individually. The whole family will need to be involved. If you have birth children they will need a chance to think about what fostering will mean for them. Confidential enquiries will be made of your local authority and the police and you will probably be asked to have a medical examination. The local authority to which you have applied will consider a report on your application and decide whether you should be approved as a foster carer or not. This process usually takes several months.

| What are the rules for looking | after children in foster care?

- The local authority must visit the home, make enquiries about the prospective foster carers and approve the foster family.

- The agency's social worker must visit the child at certain intervals.

- The local authority must keep records of foster children and foster carers. The local authority and foster carers must make a foster placement agreement, when a child is placed, about certain matters such as the arrangement for the child's health, contact with the child's birth family and financial support for the child.

- The local authority must provide foster carers with written information about such things as the child's background, health, and mental and emotional development.

> **When we first fostered young children we used to get very attached to them; secretly we hoped that we could adopt them. Now we realise that our role is to help these children go back to their parents or move on to their adoptive families. Even so, it can be pretty heart-wrenching at times.**

- The local authority must make a foster care agreement with you when you are approved. This covers expectations of both parties and includes the requirement, laid down in regulations, that you should not administer corporal punishment.

Residence Orders in Scotland

In Scotland, anyone, including foster carers, can apply for a Residence Order, if they can show that this is in the child's interests. A Residence Order gives the carers parental responsibilities and rights but not as many as an Adoption Order would and without removing all the birth parent's responsibilities and rights. A Residence Order lasts until the child is 16. The local authority can pay a Residence Order allowance but is not obliged to do so. Your local social work department can tell you more about the orders.

Residence Orders in England and Wales and Northern Ireland

The making of a Residence Order under the Children Act 1989 or Children's (NI) Order 1995 gives people looking after a child more day-to-day rights than foster carers have, but not as many as adopters. The child is no longer looked after by the local authority but the birth parents are still legally involved. There are rules which limit the ability of foster carers to apply for a Residence Order if the child's parents or local authority are not in agreement. However, if a child has lived with someone for three years, that person can go to court and apply for a Residence Order, even if the local authority or parents disagree. The local authority can pay a Residence Order allowance, but is not obliged to do so. A Residence Order lasts until the child is 16 or, exceptionally, until he or she is 18. If you want to know more about Residence Orders you should talk to your local social services department or a solicitor with experience of child care law.

Finding an adoption agency

Unless you are a close relative of the child you want to adopt, you will need to go through an adoption agency. There are nearly 250 adoption agencies in England, Scotland and Wales and Northern Ireland. Most of these are based in local authority social services departments in England and Wales or social work departments in Scotland. In Northern Ireland, social services are provided by health and social services trusts commissioned by four health and social services boards. These are listed in the following pages under the name of the county, borough or council, or health board.

There are also voluntary adoption agencies: Barnardo's is an example, with offices all over the country. Some of these are linked to churches, for example, the Catholic Children's Society.

Local authority adoption agencies covering large areas tend to take applications mainly from people within their area. However, agencies which are geographically small, eg. London boroughs, often prefer not to recruit adopters from their own area as they will tend to live too close to the birth families of the children who need placement.

Voluntary adoption agencies usually cover a wider area than the local authorities do, often covering several counties. So it is worth contacting voluntary adoption agencies in counties near to your own, as well as any in it.

You are not limited to your own immediate locality, but most agencies work roughly within a 50 mile radius of their office. It is important to remember that you and your child will need help and support from the agency after placement. It is much harder for an agency to give you adequate support if they are based a long way away and you should discuss what their plans are for this before you decide to work with them.

Would it be best to apply to the local authority or to a voluntary adoption agency?

Voluntary agencies tend to be small and to specialise in adoption and fostering work. They are often able to give very good support once a child is placed with you. Local authorities are bigger and have to respond to a wide range of needs. However, they are the agencies responsible for placing children and will consider families whom they have approved first. They will normally expect you to wait for some months after you are approved for the placement of a child looked after by them and not to respond to children from other local authorities whom you may see needing a new family. Voluntary agencies will actively help you to try and find a child, through using BAAF*Link*, *Be My Parent* and other contacts. So, there can be advantages and disadvantages in working with either type of agency.

What they are looking for

All the adoption agencies listed in the following pages are looking for permanent new families for school age children, for children with disabilities and for groups of brothers and sisters. There are some black babies and toddlers who, like all other children, need parents of the same ethnicity as themselves. If you are white and would like to adopt a baby or toddler without disabilities you can contact agencies, but you must be prepared to find that lists are closed.

British Agencies for Adoption & Fostering

British Agencies for Adoption & Fostering (BAAF) has close links with most of the adoption agencies listed in this book. You are welcome to contact us for advice about the adoption process and about finding an agency. However, we do not take up adoption applications ourselves. We have several regional offices, and we have included the address and telephone number of these on the following pages.

How to find an adoption agency

On the next few pages, you will find lists of local authority and voluntary agencies in England, Scotland and Wales. These are divided into five different regions; each of these is served by BAAF offices located in that region. Agencies in Northern Ireland are also listed. There is currently no BAAF office in Northern Ireland but enquiries should go to the Southern Region office in London.

When you have found the name of one or more agencies that are reasonably near you, it may be a good idea to ring and ask for the name of the local adoption and fostering officer – then you will know who to ask for and to write to. You can contact a number of agencies at this early stage. However, you can make a firm application and enter into the preparation and assessment process with only one agency.

Unfortunately, we have not been able to include particular details about each of the agencies, for example, whether the agency occasionally needs families for white babies or whether it has a religious interest, or whether it is currently looking for foster carers only. A phone call to the agency will of course give you the necessary details. Your BAAF regional centre will also be able to help you.

ENGLAND: NORTH

BAAF
Northern Regional Centre

Offices at:

Grove Villa
82 Cardigan Road
Headingley
LEEDS
LS6 3BJ

Tel: 0113 274 4797

and

MEA House
Ellison Place
NEWCASTLE UPON TYNE
NE1 8XS

Tel: 0191 261 6600

LOCAL AUTHORITY AGENCIES

BARNSLEY METROPOLITAN BOROUGH COUNCIL
Social Services Department
Wellington House
Wellington Street
BARNSLEY
S70 1WA
Tel: 01226 772500

BLACKBURN AND DERWEN COUNCIL
Town Hall
BLACKBURN
BB1 7DY
Tel: 01254 585585

BLACKPOOL COUNCIL
Social Services Department
Town Hall
BLACKPOOL
FY1 1AD
Tel: 01253 25212

BOLTON METROPOLITAN BOROUGH COUNCIL
Family Placement Unit
Social Services Department
Le Mans Crescent
BOLTON
BL1 1SA
Tel: 01204 522311

BRADFORD METROPOLITAN COUNCIL, CITY OF
Adoption and Fostering Unit
2nd Floor
Olicana House
Chapel Street
BRADFORD
BD1 5RE
Tel: 01274 752918

BURY, METROPOLITAN BOROUGH OF
Social Services Department
Family Placement Department
18-20 St Mary's Place
BURY
BL9 0DZ
Tel: 0161 705 5458

CALDERDALE, METROPOLITAN BOROUGH OF
Horsfall House
Skircoat Moor Road
HALIFAX
HX3 0HJ
Tel: 01422 241138

CHESHIRE COUNTY COUNCIL
Social Services Department
Goldsmith House
Hamilton Place
CHESTER
CH1 1SE
Tel: 01244 603400

CUMBRIA COUNTY COUNCIL
Social Services Department
3 Victoria Place
CARLISLE
CA1 1EH
Tel: 01228 607080

DARLINGTON COUNCIL
Social Services Department
Town Hall
DARLINGTON
DL1 5QT
Tel: 01325 380651

DONCASTER METROPOLITAN BOROUGH COUNCIL
Social Services Department
PO Box 251
The Council House
DONCASTER
DN1 3AG
Tel: 01302 737777

DURHAM COUNTY COUNCIL
Social Services Department
31 Upper Beveridge Way
Newton Aycliffe
DURHAM
DL5 4EB
Tel: 01325 311593

EAST RIDING OF YORKSHIRE COUNCIL
Family Placement Service
31/31A Lairgate
BEVERLEY
HU17 8HL
Tel: 01482 885339

GATESHEAD METROPOLITAN BOROUGH COUNCIL
Family Placement Unit
Civic Buildings
Prince Consort Road
GATESHEAD
NE8 4HJ
Tel: 0191 477 1616

HALTON BOROUGH COUNCIL
Grosvenore House
Halton Leas
RUNCORN
WA7 1LE
Tel: 0151 424 2061

HARTLEPOOL BOROUGH COUNCIL
Social Services Department
Aneurin Bevan House
Avenue Road
HARTLEPOOL
TS24 8HD
Tel: 01429 266522

ISLE OF MAN
Social Services Division
Hilary House
Prospect Hill
DOUGLAS
IM1 1EQ
Tel: 01624 686180

KINGSTON UPON HULL CITY COUNCIL
Social Services Department
Brunswick House
Strand Close
HULL
HU2 9DB
Tel: 01482 616163

KIRKLEES METROPOLITAN COUNCIL
Family Placement & Reception Unit
Oakmead
1c Lidget Street
Lindley
HUDDERSFIELD
HD3 3JB
Tel: 01484 222080

KNOWSLEY, METROPOLITAN BOROUGH OF
Social Services Department
Astley House
1 Astley Road
HUYTON
L36 8HY
Tel: 0151 443 3956

LANCASHIRE COUNTY COUNCIL
Social Services Headquarters
East Cliff County Offices
PRESTON
PR1 3EA
Tel: 01772 254868

LEEDS CITY COUNCIL
Social Services Department
Selectapost
Fostering and Adoption
4th Floor West
Merrion House
LEEDS
LS2 8QA
Tel: 0113 2478590

LIVERPOOL, CITY OF
Social Services Directorate
Sefton Grange
Croxteth Drive
LIVERPOOL
L17 3EZ
Tel: 0151 227 3911

MANCHESTER CITY COUNCIL
Chorlton Social Services Office
102 Manchester Road
MANCHESTER
M21 OPQ
Tel: 0161 881 0911

MIDDLESBROUGH BOROUGH COUNCIL
West Point
2 Cambridge Road
MIDDLESBROUGH
TS5 5NA
Tel: 01642 823727

**NEWCASTLE UPON TYNE,
CITY OF**
Social Services Department
Adoption & Fostering Unit
1 St. James Terrace
NEWCASTLE UPON TYNE
NE1 4NE
Tel: 0191 261 8124

**NORTH EAST LINCOLNSHIRE
COUNCIL**
The Annexe
The Grove
38 West Street
SCAWBY
DN20 9AN
Tel: 01652 654011

**NORTH LINCOLNSHIRE
COUNCIL**
The Annexe
The Grove
38 West Street
SCAWBY
DN20 9AN
Tel: 01652 654011

NORTH TYNESIDE COUNCIL
Fostering and Adoption
Children's Services
Camden House
Camden Street
NORTH SHIELDS
NE30 1NW
Tel: 0191 200 6161

**NORTH YORKSHIRE COUNTY
COUNCIL**
Social Services Department
County Hall
NORTHALLERTON
DL7 8DD
Tel: 01609 780780

**NORTHUMBERLAND COUNTY
COUNCIL**
Family Placement & Support Service
Tweed House
Hepscott Park
STANNINGTON
NE61 2NF
Tel: 01670 534450

**OLDHAM, METROPOLITAN
BOROUGH OF**
Fostering & Adoption Team
117 Union Street
OLDHAM
OL1 1RU
Tel: 0161 652 0322

**REDCAR & CLEVELAND
BOROUGH COUNCIL**
Grosmont Resource Centre
20 Grosmont Close
REDCAR
TS10 4PJ
Tel: 01642 495910

**ROCHDALE METROPOLITAN
BOROUGH COUNCIL**
Family Placement Team
Foxholes House
Foxholes Road
ROCHDALE
OL12 0ED
Tel: 01706 47474

**ROTHERHAM BOROUGH
COUNCIL**
Family Care Unit
Brooklands
Doncaster Road
ROTHERHAM
S65 1NN
Tel: 01709 382121

SALFORD CITY COUNCIL
Social Services Department
Avon House
Avon Close
Little Hulton
SALFORD
M28 0LA
Tel: 0161 799 1762

SEFTON, METROPOLITAN BOROUGH OF
Social Services Department
Litherland Town Hall
Sefton Road
Litherland
LIVERPOOL
L21 7PD
Tel: 0151 922 4040

SHEFFIELD METROPOLITAN CITY
Council
Family and Community Services Dept
Redvers House
Union Street
SHEFFIELD
S1 2JQ
Tel: 0114 2734811

SOUTH TYNESIDE, METROPOLITAN BOROUGH OF
Family Placements Unit
Boker Lane
EAST BOLDON
NE36 0RY
Tel: 0191 536 7241

ST HELENS, METROPOLITAN BOROUGH OF
Family Placement Team
73 Corporation Street
ST. HELENS
WA10 1SX
Tel: 01744 456000

STOCKPORT METROPOLITAN BOROUGH COUNCIL
Social Services Department
1 Baker Street
Heaton Norris
STOCKPORT
SK4 1QQ
Tel: 0161 480 7181

STOCKTON-ON-TEES BOROUGH COUNCIL
Council Offices
Town Centre
BILLINGHAM
TS23 2LW
Tel: 01642 397139

SUNDERLAND, CITY OF
Social Services Department
50 Fawcett Street
SUNDERLAND
SR1 1RF
Tel: 0191 553 7276

TAMESIDE METROPOLITAN BOROUGH
Council
Fostering and Adoption Section
12 Astley Road
STALYBRIDGE
SK15 1RA
Tel: 0161 304 9729

TRAFFORD METROPOLITAN BOROUGH COUNCIL
10 Langham Road
BOWDEN
WA14 2HU
Tel: 0161 928 1908

WAKEFIELD METROPOLITAN DISTRICT COUNCIL, CITY OF
Community & Social Services Dept
Flanshaw Children's Centre
6 Springfield Grange
Flanshaw
WAKEFIELD
WF2 9QP
Tel: 01924 302160

WARRINGTON BOROUGH COUNCIL
Bewsey Old School
Locton, Bewsey
WARRINGTON
WA5 4BF
Tel: 01925 444400

WIGAN METROPOLITAN BOROUGH COUNCIL
Social Services Department
Ince Town Hall
Ince Green Lane, Ince
WIGAN
WN3 4QX
Tel: 01942 244991

WIRRAL, METROPOLITAN BOROUGH OF
Department of Social Services
Conway Building
Burlington Street
BIRKENHEAD
L41 4FD
Tel: 0151 647 7000

YORK CITY COUNCIL
Community Services
Hollycroft
Wenlock Terrace
Fulford Road
YORK
YO1 4DU
Tel: 01904 555300

VOLUNTARY AGENCIES

BARNARDO'S NEW FAMILIES PROJECT
43 Briggate
SHIPLEY
West Yorkshire
BD17 7BP
Tel: 01274 532852

BARNARDO'S NEWCASTLE NEW FAMILIES
North East Divisional Office
Orchard House
Fenwick Terrace
Jesmond
NEWCASTLE UPON TYNE
NE2 2JQ
Tel: 0191 281 5024

BLACKBURN DIOCESAN ADOPTION AGENCY
St Mary's House
Cathedral Close
BLACKBURN
Lancashire   BB1 5AA
Tel: 01254 57759

CATHOLIC CARE (DIOCESE OF LEEDS)
31 Moor Road
Headingley
LEEDS
LS6 4BG
Tel: 0113 2787500

CATHOLIC CARE (NORTH EAST)
St Cuthberts House
West Road
NEWCASTLE UPON TYNE
NE15 7PY
Tel: 0191 228 0111

**CATHOLIC CARING SERVICES
TO CHILDREN & COMMUNITY
(LANCASTER)**
218 Tulketh Road
Ashton
PRESTON
Lancashire PR2 lES
Tel: 01772 732313

**CATHOLIC CHILDREN'S RESCUE
SOCIETY
(DIOCESE OF SALFORD)**
390 Parrs Wood Road
Didsbury
MANCHESTER
M20 ONA
Tel: 0161 445 7741

**CATHOLIC CHILDREN'S
SOCIETY
(DIOCESE OF SHREWSBURY)**
111 Shrewsbury Road
BIRKENHEAD
Merseyside
L43 8SS
Tel: 0151 652 1281

**CHESTER DIOCESAN ADOPTION
SERVICES**
14 Liverpool Road
CHESTER
CH2 lAE
Tel: 01244 390938

**DONCASTER ADOPTION &
FAMILY WELFARE SOCIETY LTD**
Jubilee House
1 Jubilee Road
Wheatley
DONCASTER
South Yorkshire
DN1 2UE
Tel: 01302 349909

**DURHAM DIOCESAN FAMILY
WELFARE COUNCIL**
Agriculture House
Stonebridge
DURHAM
DH1 3RY
Tel: 0191 386 3719

**MANCHESTER ADOPTION
SOCIETY**
47 Bury New Road
Sedgley Park
Prestwich
MANCHESTER
M25 9JY
Tel: 0161 773 0973

**NCH ACTION FOR CHILDREN
FAMILY FINDERS (NORTH EAST)**
11 Queen's Square
LEEDS
LS2 8AJ
Tel: 0113 2429631

NUGENT CARE SOCIETY
Blackbrook House
Blackbrook Road
ST HELENS
Merseyside WA11 9RJ
Tel: 01744 6057006

ENGLAND: CENTRAL

BAAF
Central Regional Centre
St George's House
Coventry Road
Coleshill
BIRMINGHAM
B46 3EA

Tel: 01675 463998

LOCAL AUTHORITY AGENCIES

BIRMINGHAM CITY COUNCIL
Social Services Department
Louisa Ryland House
44 Newhall Street
BIRMINGHAM
B3 3PL
Tel: 0121 235 2946

COVENTRY CITY COUNCIL
Social Services Department
The Grange
Brownshill Green Road
Keresley
COVENTRY
CV1 6QE
Tel: 01203 338528

DERBY CITY COUNCIL
Social Services Department
Council House
Corporation Street
DERBY
DE1 2FX
Tel: 01332 293111

DERBYSHIRE COUNTY COUNCIL
Social Services Department
County Hall
MATLOCK
DE4 3AG
Tel: 01629 580000

DUDLEY METROPOLITAN BOROUGH COUNCIL
Social Services Department
Ednam House
1 St. James's Road
DUDLEY
DY1 3JJ
Tel: 01384 818181

HEREFORDSHIRE COUNCIL
Bath Street
HEREFORD
HR1 2HQ
Tel: 01432 364 500

LEICESTER CITY COUNCIL
Social Services Department
1 Grey Friars
LEICESTER
LE1 5PH
Tel: 0116 2531191

LEICESTERSHIRE COUNTY COUNCIL
Social Services Department
Adoption Team
6 St Martins
LEICESTER
LE1 5DB
Tel: 0116 2568217

LINCOLNSHIRE COUNTY COUNCIL
Social Services Department
Wigford House
Brayford Wharf East
LINCOLN
LN5 7BH
Tel: 01522 552222

NORTHAMPTONSHIRE COUNTY COUNCIL
Social Services Department
John Dryden House
PO Box 225 Street
NORTHAMPTON
NN4 7DF
Tel: 01604 236236

NOTTINGHAM CITY COUNCIL
City District Office
Denewood Centre
Denewood Crescent
NOTTINGHAM
NG8 3DH
Tel: 0115 9157012

NOTTINGHAMSHIRE COUNTY COUNCIL
Central Adoption & Fostering Unit
The Lindens
379 Woodborough Road
NOTTINGHAM
NG3 5GX
Tel: 0115 9774616

RUTLAND COUNCIL
Social Services & Housing Dept
Catmose
OAKHAM
LE15 6HP
Tel: 01572 722577

SANDWELL METROPOLITAN BOROUGH COUNCIL
Home Finding Team South
The Hollies Family Centre
Coopers Lane
Smethwick
WARLEY
B58 3NJ
Tel: 0121 569 5770

SHROPSHIRE COUNTY COUNCIL
The County Adoption Team
Observer House
Abbey Foregate
SHREWSBURY
SY2 5DE
Tel: 01743 241915

SOLIHULL, METROPOLITAN BOROUGH OF
c/o Juvenile Centre
8 Craig Croft
Chelmsley Wood
BIRMINGHAM
B37 7TR
Tel: 0121 788 4200

STAFFORDSHIRE COUNTY COUNCIL
Social Services Department
St Chads Place
STAFFORD
ST16 2LR
Tel: 01785 276932

STOKE ON TRENT CITY COUNCIL
Social Services Department
Civic Centre
Glebe Street
STOKE ON TRENT
ST4 1RJ
Tel: 01332 293111

WALSALL METROPOLITAN BOROUGH COUNCIL
Homefinding for Children
106 Essington Road
WILLENHALL
WV12 4DT
Tel: 01922 652700

WARWICKSHIRE COUNTY COUNCIL
Social Services Department
District Office
Arden House
Masons Road
STRATFORD-UPON-AVON
CV37 9NW
Tel: 01926 410410

WOLVERHAMPTON BOROUGH COUNCIL
Children's Services
Beldray
66 Mount Pleasant
Bilston
WOLVERHAMPTON
WV14 7PR
Tel: 01902 27811

WORCESTER COUNTY COUNCIL
Children's Services
Social Services Department
County Hall
Spetchley Road
WORCESTER
WR5 2NP
Tel: 01905 763763

WREKIN COUNCIL
Social Services Department
Derby House
TELFORD
TF3 4LA
Tel: 01952 202264

VOLUNTARY AGENCIES

BARNARDO'S MIDLANDS NEW FAMILIES
Owen House
Little Cornbow
HALESOWEN
West Midlands
B63 3AJ
Tel: 0121 550 4737

CATHOLIC CHILDREN'S SOCIETY (NOTTINGHAMSHIRE)
7 Colwick Road
West Bridgford
NOTTINGHAM
NG2 5FR
Tel: 0115 955881

FATHER HUDSON'S SOCIETY
Coventry Road
Coleshill
BIRMINGHAM
B46 3ED
Tel: 01675 462816

LDS SOCIAL SERVICES (THE CHURCH OF JESUS CHRIST OF LATTER DAY SAINTS)
399 Garretts Green Lane
Garretts Green
BIRMINGHAM
B33 OUH
Tel: 0121 784 9266

NCH ACTION FOR CHILDREN FAMILY FINDERS (MIDLANDS)
Wood End Mews
141 Wood End Lane
Urdington
BIRMINGHAM
B24 8BD
Tel: 0121 377 7999

SOUTHWELL DIOCESAN COUNCIL FOR FAMILY CARE
Warren House
Pelham Court
Pelham Road
NOTTINGHAM
NG5 1AP
Tel: 0115 9603010

ENGLAND: SOUTH

BAAF Southern Regional Centre

Skyline House
200 Union Street
LONDON
SE1 OLX

Tel: 0171 593 2041

LOCAL AUTHORITY AGENCIES

BARKING & DAGENHAM, LONDON BOROUGH OF
Social Services Department
Civic Centre
DAGENHAM
RM10 7BW
Tel: 0181 592 4500

BARNET, LONDON BOROUGH OF
Family Placement
3rd Floor
Barnet House
1255 High Road
Whetstone
LONDON
N20 0EJ
Tel: 0181 359 2000

BATH AND NORTH EAST SOMERSET COUNCIL
7 North Parade Buildings
BATH
BA1 1NY
Tel: 01225 477000

BEDFORDSHIRE COUNTY COUNCIL
Social Services Department
Houghton Close
AMPTHILL
MK42 2TG
Tel: 01525 840543

BEXLEY COUNCIL
Social Services Department
Howlbury Centre
Slade Green Road
ERITH
DA8 2HX
Tel: 0181 303 7777

**BOURNEMOUTH BOROUGH
COUNCIL**
Social Services Directorate
Oxford House
BOURNEMOUTH
BH8 8HA
Tel: 01202 446500

**BRACKNELL FOREST
BOROUGH COUNCIL**
Family Placement Team
Time Square
Market Street
BRACKNELL
RG12 1JD
Tel: 01344 424642

BRENT, LONDON BOROUGH OF
Brent Family Placements Services
Triangle House
328-330 High Road
WEMBLEY
HA9 6AZ
Tel: 0181 937 1234

BRIGHTON AND HOVE COUNCIL
Social Services Department
King's House
Grand Avenue
HOVE
BN3 2LS
Tel: 01273 290000

BRISTOL CITY COUNCIL
Social Services Department
Avon House
PO Box 30
The Haymarket
BRISTOL
BS99 7NB
Tel: 0117 9871100

**BROMLEY,
LONDON BOROUGH OF**
Social Services Department
Joseph Lancaster Hall
Civic Centre
Rafford Way
BROMLEY
BR1 3UH
Tel: 0181 464 3333

**BUCKINGHAMSHIRE
COUNTY COUNCIL**
Social Services Department
King George V Road
AMERSHAM
HP6 5BN
Tel: 01494 729000

**CAMBRIDGESHIRE
COUNTY COUNCIL**
HomefindersCentre
Buttsgrove Centre
38 Buttsgrove Way
HUNTINGDON
PE18 7LY
Tel: 01480 386404

CAMDEN, LONDON BOROUGH OF
Permanent Placement Team
Gospel Oak Office
115 Wellesley Road
LONDON
NW5 4PA
Tel: 0171 413 6666

CITY OF LONDON
Social Services Department
Milton Court
Moor Lane
LONDON
EC2Y 9BL
Tel: 0171 332 1219

CORNWALL COUNTY COUNCIL
Adoption & Family Finding Unit
13 Treyew Road
TRURO
TR1 2BY
Tel: 01872 70251

**CROYDON,
LONDON BOROUGH OF**
Family Placements Unit
Social Services Department
130 Brighton Road
PURLEY
CR8 4HA
Tel: 0181 660 4844

DEVON COUNTY COUNCIL
Social Services Department
Room A126
County Hall
Topsham Road
EXETER
EX2 4QR
Tel: 01392 382000

DORSET COUNTY COUNCIL
County Hall
DORCHESTER
DT1 1XJ
Tel: 01305 251000

EALING, LONDON BOROUGH OF
Social Services Department
Family Placement Services
Acton Town Hall
Winchester Street
Acton
LONDON
W3 6NE
Tel: 0181 579 2424

EAST SUSSEX COUNTY COUNCIL
Social Services Department
Children and Families Division
PO Box 5
St Anne's Crescent
County Hall
LEWIS
BN7 1SW
Tel: 01273 481233

ENFIELD, LONDON BOROUGH OF
Southgate Town Hall
Green Lanes
Palmers Green
LONDON
N13 4XD
Tel: 0181 366 6565

ESSEX COUNTY COUNCIL
Social Services Department
PO Box 297
County Hall
CHELMSFORD
CM1 1YS
Tel: 01245 492211

**EXETER DIOCESE BOARD FOR
CHRISTIAN CARE (FAMILIES
FOR CHILDREN)**
Glenn House
96 Old Tiverton Road
EXETER
EX4 6LD
Tel: 01392 278875

**GLOUCESTERSHIRE COUNTY
COUNCIL**
Social Services Department
Shire Hall
Westgate Street
GLOUCESTER
GL1 2TR
Tel: 01452 425100

GREENWICH, LONDON BOROUGH OF
147 Powis Street
LONDON
SE18 6JL
Tel: 0181 854 8888

GUERNSEY, STATES OF
Children Board
Homefinding Unit
Garden Hill Resource Centre
Swissville
Rohais
St. Peter Port
GUERNSEY
Channel Islands GY1 1FB
Tel: 01481 713230

HACKNEY, LONDON BOROUGH OF
Young Person's Resource Centre
23/25 Sutton Place
LONDON
E9 6EH
Tel: 0181 986 3123

HAMMERSMITH AND FULHAM, LONDON BOROUGH OF
Hammersmith Town Hall Extension
1st Floor
King Street
Hammersmith
LONDON
W6 9JU
Tel: 0181 748 3020

HAMPSHIRE COUNTY COUNCIL
Social Services Department
Trafalgar House
The Castle
WINCHESTER
SO23 8UQ
Tel: 01962 847176

HARINGEY COUNCIL
Children & Adult Provider Service
Grosvenor House
27 The Broadway
Crouch End
LONDON
N8 8DU
Tel: 0181 975 9700

HARROW, LONDON BOROUGH OF
Family Placement Unit
Social Services Department
427-433 Pinner Road
HARROW
HA1 4HN
Tel: 0181 863 5611

HAVERING, LONDON BOROUGH OF
Family Placement Team
Whitworth Centre
Noak Hill Road
Harold Hill
ROMFORD
RM3 7YA
Tel: 01708 772222

HERTFORDSHIRE COUNTY COUNCIL
Family Placement Service (Long Term)
120 Victoria Street
ST ALBANS
AL1 3TG
Tel: 01727 866505

HILLINGDON, LONDON BOROUGH OF
Residential & Family Placement Team
Moorcroft Complex
Harlington Road
UXBRIDGE
UB8 3HD
Tel: 01895 253377

HOUNSLOW,
LONDON BOROUGH OF
Social Services Department
London Borough of Hounslow
26 Glenhurst Road
BRENTFORD
TW8 9BX
Tel: 0181 862 6698

ISLE OF WIGHT COUNTY
COUNCIL
Sandown Neighbourhood Office
The Barrack Block
The Broadway
SANDOWN
PO36 9BS
Tel: 01983 408448

ISLINGTON,
LONDON BOROUGH OF
Permanence Family Placement Team
29 Highbury New Park
LONDON
N5 2EN
Tel: 0171 704 1997

JERSEY, STATES OF
Children's Service
Maison Le Pape
Saville Street
St Helier
JERSEY
Channel Islands
JE2 3XF
Tel: 01534 870600

KENSINGTON & CHELSEA,
ROYAL BOROUGH OF
Family Placement Unit
2 Allen Street
LONDON
W8 6BH
Tel: 0171 937 7290

KENT COUNTY COUNCIL
Social Services Department
Joynes House
New Road
GRAVESEND
DA1 0AT
Tel: 01474 328664

KINGSTON UPON THAMES,
ROYAL BOROUGH OF
Community Services Department
Family Placement Team
Guildhall
High Street
KINGSTON UPON THAMES
KT1 1EU
Tel: 0181 547 6042

LAMBETH,
LONDON BOROUGH OF
Family Finders
392-394 Brixton Road
LONDON
SW9 7AW
Tel: 0171 926 8500

LEWISHAM,
LONDON BOROUGH OF
Fostering and Adoption Unit
Hollydale
43-45 Bromley Road
LONDON
SE6 2UA
Tel: 0181 695 6000

LUTON COUNCIL
Social Services Department
Unity House
111 Stuart Street
LUTON
LU1 5NP
Tel: 01582 546000

MEDWAY TOWNS COUNCIL
Social Services
Compass Centre
Pembroke
Chatham Maritime
CHATHAM
ME4 4YH
Tel: 01634 880404

MERTON, LONDON BOROUGH OF
Adoption and Fostering Team/
Community Fostering Teams
Social Services Division
Worsford House
MITCHAM
CR4 3BE
Tel: 0181 545 2222

MILTON KEYNES COUNCIL
Neighbourhood Services Directorate
Saxon Court
502 Avebury Boulevard
MILTON KEYNES
MK9 3HS
Tel: 01908 691691

NEWBURY COUNCIL
West Berkshire Social Services
Pelican House
9-15 West Street
NEWBURY
RG14 1BZ
Tel: 01635 46545

**NEWHAM,
LONDON BOROUGH OF**
Social Services Department
Broadway House
Stratford
LONDON
E15 1AJ
Tel: 0181 534 4545

NORFOLK COUNTY COUNCIL
Adoption and Family Finding Unit
3 Unthank Road
NORWICH
NR2 2PA
Tel: 01603 617796

NORTH SOMERSET DISTRICT COUNCIL
Social Services Department
Town Hall
WESTON-SUPER-MARE
BS23 1ZY
Tel: 01934 634803

OXFORDSHIRE COUNTY COUNCIL
Children and Families
Social Services Department
Yarnton House
Rutten Lane
OXFORD
OX5 1LP
Tel: 01865 854400

PETERBOROUGH CITY COUNCIL
Broadway
PETERBOROUGH
PE1 1HU
Tel: 01733 63141

PLYMOUTH CITY COUNCIL (UNITARY)
Civic Centre
Royal Parade
PLYMOUTH
PL1 2EW
Tel: 01752 668000

POOLE BOROUGH COUNCIL
Adoption and Fostering Team
Children and Families Services
14A Commercial Road
Parkstone
POOLE
BH14 OJW
Tel: 01202 633633

PORTSMOUTH CITY COUNCIL
c/o Hampshire Social Services
The Castle
WINCHESTER
SO23 8UQ
Tel: 01962 847176

READING BOROUGH COUNCIL
Family Placement Team
Abbey Mill House
Abbey Square
READING
RG1 3BE
Tel: 0118 9586111

REDBRIDGE, LONDON BOROUGH OF
Family Placements
235 Grove Road
CHADWELL HEATH
RM6 4XD
Tel: 0181 478 3020

RICHMOND UPON THAMES, LONDON BOROUGH OF
Children's Division
Social Services Department
42 York Street
TWICKENHAM
TW1 3BW
Tel: 081 891 7654

SLOUGH BOROUGH COUNCIL
Family Placement Team
New High Field
Wexham Road
SLOUGH
SL1 1AS
Tel: 01753 690400

SOMERSET COUNTY COUNCIL
Social Services Department
County Hall
TAUNTON
TA1 4DY
Tel: 01823 355455

SOUTH GLOUCESTERSHIRE COUNCIL
Social Services Department
2A Newton Road
Cadbury Heath
BRISTOL
BS15 5EZ
Tel: 01454 416262

SOUTHAMPTON CITY COUNCIL
Social Services Department
Southbrook Rise
Millbrook Road East
SOUTHAMPTON
SO15 1YG
Tel: 01703 833101

SOUTHEND COUNCIL
PO Box 6
Civic Centre
Victoria Avenue
SOUTHEND-ON-SEA
SS2 6ER
Tel: 01702 215000

**SOUTHWARK, LONDON
BOROUGH OF**
Adoption & Fostering Unit
27-29 Camberwell Road
LONDON
SE5 0EZ
Tel: 0171 525 5991

SUFFOLK COUNTY COUNCIL
Social Services Department
St. Paul House
County Hall
IPSWICH
IP4 1LH
Tel: 01473 583400

SURREY COUNTY COUNCIL
County Children & Families Service
Beaufort House
Mayford Green
WOKING
GU22 0PG
Tel: 01483 728022

SUTTON, LONDON BOROUGH OF
Family Placement Team
314 Malden Road
Cheam
SUTTON
SM3 8EP
Tel: 0181 770 4480

SWINDON BOROUGH COUNCIL
Social Services Department
Civic Offices
Euclid Street
SWINDON
SN1 2JL
Tel: 01793 463000

THURROCK COUNCIL
Civic Office
New Road
GRAYS
RM17 6SL
Tel: 01375 390000

TORBAY BOROUGH COUNCIL
Civic Offices
Council Circus
TORQUAY
TQ1 3DR
Tel: 01803 296244

**TOWER HAMLETS,
LONDON BOROUGH OF**
Family Placement Service
62 Roman Road
Bethnal Green
LONDON
E2 0QJ
Tel: 0171 364 5000

**WALTHAM FOREST,
LONDON BOROUGH OF**
Families Placement Unit
8 Oliver Road
LONDON
E10 5JY
Tel: 0181 539 9797

**WANDSWORTH,
LONDON BOROUGH OF**
Adoption & Fostering Unit
Welbeck House
43-51 Wandsworth High Street
LONDON
SW18 2PU
Tel: 0181 871 7261

WEST SUSSEX COUNTY COUNCIL
Children's Services Unit
Grange Block
Tower Street
CHICHESTER
PO19 1QT
Tel: 01243 777683

WESTMINSTER, CITY OF
Family Placements
33 Tachbrook Street
LONDON
SW1V 2JR
Tel: 0171 641 3186

WILTSHIRE COUNTY COUNCIL
Children's Resource Centre
357 Hungerdown Lane
CHIPPENHAM
SN14 0UY
Tel: 01249 460222

**WINDSOR AND MAIDENHEAD
AUTHORITY, ROYAL BOROUGH
OF**
Family Placement Team
4 Marlow Road
MAIDENHEAD
SL2 7YR
Tel: 01628 798888

**WOKINGHAM DISTRICT
COUNCIL AUTHORITY**
Family Placement Team
Wellington House
Wellington Road
WOKINGHAM
RG40 2QB
Tel: 01189 789656

VOLUNTARY AGENCIES

BARNARDO'S (HEAD OFFICE)
Tanners Lane
Barkingside
ILFORD
IG6 1QG
Tel: 0181 550 8822

BARNARDO'S JIGSAW PROJECT
12 Church Hill
Walthamstow
LONDON
E17 3AG
Tel: 0181 521 0033

**BARNARDO'S NEW FAMILIES
PROJECT**
54 Head Street
COLCHESTER
C01 1PB
Tel: 01206 562438

**CATHOLIC CHILDREN'S
SOCIETY (ARUNDEL &
BRIGHTON, PORTSMOUTH &
SOUTHWARK)**
49 Russell Hill Road
PURLEY
Surrey
CR8 2XB
Tel: 0181 6682181

**CATHOLIC CHILDREN'S
SOCIETY
(DIOCESE OF CLIFTON)**
58 Alma Road
Clifton
BRISTOL
BS8 2DQ
Tel: 0117 9734253

**Catholic Children's Society
(Littlehampton)**
53 Arundel Road
LITTLEHAMPTON
BN17 7BY
Tel: 01903 715317

**Catholic Children's Society
(Gravesend)**
28 Leith Road
GRAVESEND
DA12 1LW
Tel: 01474 325521

**Catholic Children's Society
(Southampton)**
57 Lodge Road
SOUTHAMPTON
SO14 6RL
Tel: 01703 229129

**Catholic Children's Society
(Winchester)**
7 Bridge Street
WINCHESTER
SO23 8HN
Tel: 01962 842024

**CATHOLIC CHILDREN'S
SOCIETY (WESTMINSTER)
CRUSADE OF RESCUE**
73 St Charles' Square
LONDON
W10 6EJ
Tel: 0181 969 5305

CHILDLINK ADOPTION SOCIETY
10 Lion Yard
Tremadoc Road
LONDON
SW4 7NQ
Tel: 0171 498 1933

**THE CHILDREN'S SOCIETY
(HEAD OFFICE)**
Public Enquiry Unit
Edward Rudolf House
69-89 Margery Street
LONDON
WC1X 0JL
Tel: 0171 837 4299

**FAMILIES FOR CHILDREN
(EXETER DIOCESE BOARD FOR
CHRISTIAN CARE)**
Glenn House
96 Old Tiverton Road
EXETER
EX4 6LD
Tel: 01392 278875

**INDEPENDENT ADOPTION
SERVICE**
121-123 Camberwell Road
LONDON
SE5 0HB
Tel: 0171 703 1088

**NCH ACTION FOR CHILDREN
(HEAD OFFICE)**
85 Highbury Park
LONDON
N5 1UD
Tel: 0171 226 2033

NCH ACTION FOR CHILDREN
Adoption & Fostering Resources Team
Horner Court
637 Gloucester Road
Horfield
BRISTOL
BS7 OBJ
Tel: 0117 9354580

NCH ACTION FOR CHILDREN
ASHWOOD PROJECT (Homefinding)
158 Crawley Road
Roffey
HORSHAM
West Sussex
RH12 4EU
Tel: 01403 225900

NORWOOD JEWISH ADOPTION SOCIETY
Family Placement Service
Norwood House
Harmony Way
off Victoria Road
LONDON
NW4 2BZ
Tel: 0181 203 3030

PARENTS AND CHILDREN TOGETHER (PACT)
48 Bath Road
READING
Berkshire
RG1 6PG
Tel: 01189 581861

PARENTS FOR CHILDREN
41 Southgate Road
LONDON
N1 3JP
Tel: 0171 359 7530

ST FRANCIS' CHILDREN'S SOCIETY
64 Gardenia Avenue
LUTON
LU3 2NS
Tel: 01582 492277

ST FRANCIS' CHILDREN'S SOCIETY
Northants and North Bucks Office
20A Park Avenue North
NORTHAMPTON
NN3 2HS
Tel: 01604 715202

THE SOLDIERS', SAILORS' AND AIRMEN'S FAMILIES ASSOCIATION (SSAFA) FORCES HELP
Queen Elizabeth the Queen Mother House
19 Queen Elizabeth Street
LONDON
SE1 2LP
Tel: 0171 403 8783

THOMAS CORAM FOUNDATION FOR CHILDREN
40 Brunswick Square
LONDON
WC1N 1AZ
Tel: 0171 278 2424

WALES

BAAF Welsh Centre
7 Cleeve House
Lambourne Crescent
CARDIFF
CF4 5GJ

Tel: 01222 761155

LOCAL AUTHORITY AGENCIES

ANGLESEY COUNTY COUNCIL, ISLE OF
Social Services Department
Shire Hall
Glanhwfa Road
LLANGEFNI
LL77 7TS
Tel: 01248 752733

COUNTY BOROUGH OF BLAENAU GWENT
Social Services Department
107/110 Worcester Street
BRYNMAWR
NP3 4JP
Tel: 01495 313803

BRIDGEND COUNTY BOROUGH COUNCIL
Bridgend Personal Services
Directorate
County Offices
Sunnyside
BRIDGEND
CF31 4AR
Tel: 01656 642200

CAERPHILLY COUNTY BOROUGH COUNCIL
Social Services & Housing
Directorate
Hawtin Park
Gellihaf
Blackwood
PONTLLANFRAITH
NP2 2PZ
Tel: 01443 815588

CARDIFF COUNTY COUNCIL
Children's Services
Trowbridge Centre
Greenway Road
CARDIFF
CF3 8QS
Tel: 01222 774600

CARMARTHENSHIRE COUNTY COUNCIL
Social Services Department
3 Spilman Street
CARMARTHEN
SA31 1LE
Tel: 01267 234567

CEREDIGION COUNTY COUNCIL
Social Services Department
Headquarters
Min Aeron
Vicarage Hill
ABERAERON
Ceredigion SA46 0DY
Tel: 01545 570382

CONWY COUNTY BOROUGH COUNCIL
Family Placement Team
94 Conwy Road
Colwyn Bay
CONWY
LL29 7LE
Tel: 01492 532184

DENBIGHSHIRE COUNTY COUNCIL
Social Services Department
Cefndy Children's Resource Centre
Cefndy Road
RHYL
LL18 2HG
Tel: 01745 332468

FLINTSHIRE COUNTY COUNCIL
Social Services Department
County Offices
Civic Centre
Wepre Drive
CONNAHS QUAY
CH5 4HB
Tel: 01545 570881

VALE OF GLAMORGAN BOROUGH COUNCIL
Social Services Department
91 Salisbury Road
BARRY
CF62 6PD
Tel: 01446 745820

GWYNEDD COUNCIL
Social Services Department
Penrallt
CAERNARFON
LL55 1BN
Tel: 01286 682646

MERTHYR TYDFIL BOROUGH COUNCIL
Social Services Department
Ty Keir Hardie
Riverside Court
Avenue de Clichy
MERTHYR TYDFIL
CF47 8XE
Tel: 01685 725000

MONMOUTHSHIRE COUNTY COUNCIL
Social Services Department
Newbridge House
Tudor Street
ABERGAVENNY
NP7 5HY
Tel: 01873 859426

NEATH PORT TALBOT COUNTY BOROUGH COUNCIL
Social Services Department
The Laurels
87 Lewis Road
Port Talbot
NEATH
SA11 1DJ
Tel: 01639 765440

NEWPORT COUNTY BOROUGH COUNCIL
Social Services Department
Royal Chambers
High Street
NEWPORT
NP9 1RN
Tel: 01633 246724

PEMBROKESHIRE COUNTY COUNCIL
Family Placement Centre
The Elms
Golden Hill
PEMBROKESHIRE
SA71 4QB
Tel: 01646 683747

POWYS COUNTY COUNCIL
Social Services Department
County Hall
LLANDRINDOD WELLS
LD1 5LG
Tel: 01597 826000

RHONDDA CYNON TAFF COUNTY BOROUGH COUNCIL
The Pavilions
Cambrian Park
Clydach Vale
TONYPANDY
Rhondda Cynon Taff
CF40 2XX
Tel: 01443 424000

SWANSEA COUNTY COUNCIL
Social Services Department
Cockett House
Cockett Road
COCKETT
SWANSEA
SA2 0FJ
Tel: 01792 584622

TORFAEN COUNTY BOROUGH COUNCIL
Social Services Department
County Hall
CWMBRAN
NP44 2WN
Tel: 01633 762200

WREXHAM COUNTY BOROUGH COUNCIL
Social Services Department
3-9 Grosvenor Road
WREXHAM
LL11 1DB
Tel: 01978 291422

VOLUNTARY AGENCIES

BARNARDO'S
Derwen Family Placement Services
12 North Road
CARDIFF
CF1 3DY
Tel: 01222 387867

CATHOLIC CHILDREN AND FAMILY CARE (WALES)
Bishop Brown House
Durham Street
Grangetown
CARDIFF
CF1 7PB
Tel: 01222 667007

SCOTLAND

BAAF Scottish Centre
40 Shandwick Place
EDINBURGH
EH2 4RT

Tel: 0131 225 9285

LOCAL AUTHORITY AGENCIES

ABERDEEN CITY COUNCIL
Social Work Department
St Nicholas House
Broad Street
ABERDEEN
AB10 1BY
Tel: 01224 522000

ABERDEENSHIRE COUNCIL
Woodhill House
Westburn Road
ABERDEEN
AB16 5GB
Tel: 01224 682222

ANGUS COUNCIL
Social Work Department
Bruce House
Wellgate
ARBROATH
DD11 3TS
Tel: 01241 435096

ARGYLL AND BUTE COUNCIL
Social Work Department
Dalriada House
Lochnell Street
LOCHGILPHEAD
PA31 8ST
Tel: 01546 602177

CLACKMANNANSHIRE COUNCIL
SOCIAL WORK DEPARTMENT
BEDFORD HOUSE
13 Bedford Place
ALLOA
FK10 1LN
Tel: 01259 724336

DUMFRIES AND GALLOWAY COUNCIL
Social Work Department
Loveburn Hall
43 Newall Terrace
DUMFRIES
DG1 1LN
Tel: 01387 260357

DUNDEE CITY COUNCIL
Social Work Department
Floor 7, Tayside House
28 Crichton Street
DUNDEE
DD1 3RN
Tel: 01382 433515

EAST AYRSHIRE COUNCIL
Social Work Department
PO Box 13
Civic Centre
John Dickie Street
KILMARNOCK
KA1 1BY
Tel: 01563 576000

EAST DUNBARTONSHIRE COUNCIL
2-4 West High Street
Kirkintilloch
GLASGOW
G66 1AD
Tel: 0141 775 9000

EAST LOTHIAN COUNCIL
Social Work Centre
3 Church Street
TRANENT
EH33 1AA
Tel: 01875 615415

EAST RENFREWSHIRE COUNCIL
Social Work Department
Eagle Building, 4th Floor
15 Bothwell Street
GLASGOW
G2 7ED
Tel: 0141 577 3488

EDINBURGH COUNCIL, CITY OF
Social Work Department
Springwell House
1 Gorgie Road
EDINBURGH
EH11 3LA
Tel: 0131 313 3366

FALKIRK COUNCIL
Social Work Department
Brockville
Hope Street
FALKIRK
FK1 5RW
Tel: 01324 506400

FIFE COUNCIL
Social Work Department
Ling House
29 Canmore Street
DUNFERMLINE
KY12 7NU
Tel: 01383 312100

GLASGOW CITY COUNCIL
Family Finding Centre
115 Wellington Street
GLASGOW
G2 2XT
Tel: 0141 287 6044

HIGHLAND COUNCIL
Family Resource Centre
Limetree Avenue
INVERNESS
IV3 5RH
Tel: 01463 234120

INVERCLYDE COUNCIL
Social & Community Division
195 Dalrymple Street
GREENOCK
PA15 1UN
Tel: 01475 786811

MIDLOTHIAN COUNCIL
Social Work Department
4 Clerk Street
LOANHEAD
EH20 9DR
Tel: 0131 440 3000

MORAY COUNCIL
Social Work Department
Springfield House
Edgar Road
ELGIN
IV30 3FF
Tel: 01343 557000

NORTH AYRSHIRE COUNCIL
Elliot House
Redburn Industrial Estate
Kilwinning Road
IRVINE
KA12 8TB
Tel: 01294 317700

NORTH LANARKSHIRE COUNCIL
Social Work Department HQ
Scott House
73/77 Merry Street
MOTHERWELL
ML1 1JE
Tel: 01698 332052

ORKNEY ISLANDS COUNCIL
Children and Families Team
Social Work Department
Laing Street
KIRKWALL
Orkney KW15 1NW
Tel: 01856 870193

PERTH & KINROSS COUNCIL
Social Work Department
Rosslyn House
32 Glasgow Road
PERTH
PH2 OLG
Tel: 01738 476700

RENFREWSHIRE COUNCIL
Social Work Department
North Building
4th Floor
Cotton Street
PAISLEY
PA1 1BU
Tel: 0141 842 5158

SCOTTISH BORDERS COUNCIL
Placement Team
1 Chapel Street
SELKIRK
TD7 4JY
Tel: 01750 21926

SHETLAND ISLANDS COUNCIL
Social Work Department
92 St Olaf Street
LERWICK
Shetland ZE1 0PE
Tel: 01595 744428

SOUTH AYRSHIRE COUNCIL
Social Work Services
Holmston House
3 Holmston Road
AYR
KA7 3BA
Tel: 01292 262111

SOUTH LANARKSHIRE COUNCIL
Adoption and Fostering
Social Work Department
9 High Patrick Street
HAMILTON
ML3 7ES
Tel: 01698 455484

STIRLING COUNCIL
Social Work Department
Viewforth
STIRLING
FK8 2ET
Tel: 01786 443434

WEST DUNBARTONSHIRE COUNCIL
Social Work Department
Council Offices
Garshake Road
DUMBARTON
G82 3PU
Tel: 01389 737734

WEST LOTHIAN COUNCIL
Community Services
West Lothian House
Livingston
WEST LOTHIAN
EH54 6QG
Tel: 01506 777333

WESTERN ISLES COUNCIL
Social Work Department
Council Buildings
Rathad Shanndabhaig (Sandwick Road)
STEORNABHAGH (Stornoway)
Isle of Lewis HS1 2BW
Tel: 01851 703773

VOLUNTARY AGENCIES

BARNARDO'S FAMILY PLACEMENT SERVICES
6 Torphichen Street
EDINBURGH
EH3 8JQ
Tel: 0131 228 4121

FAMILY CARE
21 Castle Street
EDINBURGH
EH2 3DN
Tel: 0131 225 6441
Counselling Service only

ST ANDREW'S CHILDREN'S SOCIETY
Gillis Centre
113 Whitehouse Loan
EDINBURGH
EH9 1BB
Tel: 0131 452 8248

ST MARGARET OF SCOTLAND ADOPTION SOCIETY
274 Bath Street
GLASGOW
G2 4JR
Tel: 0141 332 8371

SCOTTISH ADOPTION ASSOCIATION LTD
2 Commercial Street
Leith
EDINBURGH
EH16 6JA
Tel: 0131 553 5060

NORTHERN IRELAND

BAAF does not have an office in Northern Ireland. Enquiries should be directed to:
BAAF Southern Region
200 Union Street
LONDON
SE1 0LX

Tel: 0171 593 2041

Note: Adoption and Fostering Units are located in Health and Social Services Trusts which are divided into four regional Boards.

EHSSB COMMUNITY TRUSTS

DOWN LISBURN TRUST
Warren Children's Centre
61 Woodland Park
LISBURN
BT28 1LQ
Tel: 01846 607528

ULSTER COMMUNITY AND HOSPITALS TRUST
Homefinding Team
Balloo Units
57 – 58 Dunlop Commercial Park
BANGOR
BT19 7QY
Tel: 01247 270672

NORTH & WEST BELFAST HSS TRUST
Glendinning House
6 Murray Street
BELFAST
BT1 6DP
Tel. 01232 327156

SOUTH & EAST BELFAST HSS TRUST
Adoption Services Manager
33 Wellington Park
BELFAST
BT9 6DL
Tel: 01232 683101

NHSSB COMMUNITY TRUSTS

HOMEFIRST COMMUNITY TRUST
Children's Services Directorate
Pinewood Offices
101 Fry's Road
BALLYMENA
BT43 7EN
Tel: 01266 658531

CAUSEWAY HSS TRUST
Riverside House
28 Portstewart Road
COLERAINE
BT52 1RN
Co Londonderry
Tel: 01265 58158

WHSSB COMMUNITY TRUSTS

FOYLE HSS TRUST
Riverview
Abercorn Road
LONDONDERRY
BT48 6SB
Tel: 01504 266111

SPERRIN LAKELAND HSS TRUST
Director of Community Care
Erne Hospital
Cornagrade Road
ENNISKILLEN
Co Fermanagh
Tel: 01662 244127

SHSSB COMMUNITY TRUSTS

ARMAGH & DUNGANNON HSS TRUST
Lisanally House
87 Lisanally Lane
ARMAGH
BT61 7HW
Tel: 01861 522262

CRAIGAVON BANBRIDGE HSS TRUST
Bannvale House
Moyallen Road
GILFORD
BT63 5JX
Tel: 01762 831983

NEWRY & MOURNE HSS TRUST
Butterfield House
Family Placement Team
24 Managhan Street
NEWRY
BT35 6AA
Tel: 01693 250 808

VOLUNTARY ADOPTION AGENCIES

**CHURCH OF IRELAND
ADOPTION SOCIETY**
61 – 67 Donegall Street
BELFAST
BT1 2QH
Tel: 01232 233885

FAMILY WELFARE SOCIETY
511 Ormeau Road
BELFAST
BT7 3GS
Tel: 01232 691133

USEFUL ORGANISATIONS

ADOPT
The Peskett Centre
2 Windsor Road
BELFAST
BT9 7FQ
Tel: 01232 382353

BAAF and other useful organisations

BAAF and BAAF services

British Agencies for Adoption and Fostering (BAAF)

BAAF is a registered charity and professional association for all those working in the child care field. BAAF's work includes giving advice and information to members of the public on aspects of adoption, fostering and child care issues; publishing a wide range of books, training packs and leaflets as well as a quarterly journal on adoption, fostering and child care issues; providing training and consultancy services to social workers and other professionals to help them improve the quality of medical, legal and social work services to children and families; giving evidence to govermnent committees on subjects concerning children and families; responding to consultative documents on changes in legislation and regulations affecting children in or at risk of coming into care; and helping to find new families for children through BAAF*Link* and *Be My Parent*.

Be My Parent

Every two months, nearly two hundred children waiting for new permanent families are featured in *Be My Parent*, the national family-finding newspaper published by BAAF. Subscribers to *Be My Parent* include already approved adopters, those waiting to be approved and those who have only just begun to think about adopting or permanently fostering. Children of all ages and with a wide range of needs from all over the country are featured, and therefore *Be My Parent* seeks as wide a readership as possible.

Many hundreds of families (married couples and single people) adopted after first having seen their child's photograph and read their profile in *Be My Parent*. It is easy to subscribe and have the newspaper sent directly to you – just telephone the number below. If you see children in *Be My Parent* who you would like to become part of your family, one telephone call to our staff will begin the process that could lead to you becoming approved to adopt that child.

For people already approved to adopt or permanently foster children of five and under, BAAF also publishes *Focus on Fives*. This newsletter, circulated to subscribers fortnightly, is available in the same way.

Be My Parent is at

BAAF
Skyline House
200 Union Street
London SE1 OLX

Tel: 0171 593 2060/1/2

BAAF*Link*

BAAF*Link* is a national database of children and families referred by local authorities and voluntary adoption agencies throughout Britain. Details of children needing permanent new families and of families approved by agencies are stored and links are made between the two.

BAAF*Link* seeks a variety of approved families for children needing permanent placements – couples and single people, older people and those with or without children who can reflect the cultural and religious needs of children of all ages. We particularly need black families, especially those of African-Caribbean and Asian descent, and couples in which one partner is white and one African-Caribbean. Any family referred to BAAF*Link* must be approved to adopt or permanently foster.

BAAF*Link* is at:

Mea House
Ellison Place
Newcastle-upon-Tyne
NE1 8XS
Tel: 0191 232 3200
Fax: 0191 232 2063

Scottish Resource Network

The Scottish Resource Network is a child placement service run by BAAF in Scotland. The West of Scotland Consortium facilitates the placement of children across local authority boundaries in Scotland. Information about the Scottish Resource Network and West of Scotland Consortium can be obtained from the Scottish Centre (see below).

BAAF Offices

More information about BAAF can be obtained from:

Head Office	**Scottish Centre**	**Welsh Centre**
Skyline House	40 Shandwick Place	7 Cleeve House
200 Union Street	Edinburgh EH2 4RT	Lambourne Crescent
London SE1 0LX		Cardiff CF4 5GJ
	Tel: 0131 225 9285	
Tel: 0171 593 2000	*Fax: 0131 226 3778*	*Tel: 01222 761155*
Fax: 0171 593 2001		

Regional centres are listed in Chapter 8.

Organisations for parents

AFAA (The Association for Families who have Adopted from Abroad)

AFAA
89 Upper Fant Road
Maidstone
Kent ME16 8BT
Tel: 01622 755065

Contact a Family

Contact a Family is a national charity for any parent or professional involved with or caring for a child with disabilities. Through a network of mutual support and self-help groups, Contact a Family brings together families whose children have disabilities, and offers advice and information to parents who wish to start a support group.

Contact a Family
170 Tottenham Court Road
London WlP OHA
Tel: 0171 383 3555
Fax: 0171 383 0259

Exploring Parenthood

Exploring Parenthood is an organisation which offers help and advice to parents and runs an advice line during office hours.

Exploring Parenthood
4 Ivory Place
20a Treadgold Street
London W11 4BP
Tel: 0171 221 6681
Fax: 0171 221 5501

Parent Network

Parent Network is a national charity that offers a range of courses to parents and professionals supporting families. Courses aim to enhance skills and relationships within the family, using positive, but non-violent approaches to discipline.

Parent Network
Winchester House
11 Cranmer Road
London SW9 6EJ
Tel: 0171 735 1214
Fax: 0171 735 4692

Parent to Parent Information on Adoption Services (PPIAS)

Parent to Parent Information on Adoption Services (PPIAS) is a self-help support and information service for adoptive families and prospective adopters with local support groups and contacts all over the UK. A quarterly journal, information leaflets and resource packs are available to all members.

Membership £15 per annum.

Lower Boddington
Daventry
Northants NN11 6YB
Tel: 01327 260295

Post and after adoption centres

There are many well established after adoption services now that provide a service for adoptive families, adopted people and birth parents whose children were adopted. Many of them offer advice and counselling, preferably in person, but also on the telephone or by correspondence, for individuals and families. Some also organise events which focus on matters related to adoption, and provide the opportunity for people to meet in common interest groups.

Post-Adoption Centre
Torriano Mews
Torriano Ave
London
NW5 2RZ
Tel. 0171 284 0555

After Adoption
12-14 Chapel Street
Salford
Manchester
M3 7NN
Tel. 0161 839 4930

After Adoption Yorkshire
82 Cardigan Road
Leeds
LS6 3B5
Tel. 0113 2302100

After Adoption Wales
Unit 1 Cowbridge Court
58-62 Cowbridge Road
West Cardiff
CF5 5BS
Tel. 01222 575318

West Midlands Post Adoption Service (WMPAS)
92 Newcombe Road
Handsworth
Birmingham
B21 8DD
Tel. 0121 523 3343

Merseyside Adoption Centre
316-317 Coopers Building
Church Street
Liverpool
L1 3AA
Tel. 0151 709 9122

Family Care
21 Castle Street
Edinburgh
EH2 3DN
Tel. 0131 225 6441

Barnardo's Scottish Adoption Advice Service
16 Sandyford Place
Glasgow
G3 7NB
Tel. 0141 339 0772

Local authorities may also provide help and support. In Scotland, they have a duty to help adoptive families, adopted children and birth families. They sometimes use the help of voluntary agencies for this.

Fostering

National Foster Care Association (NFCA)

National Foster Care Association (NFCA)
Leonard House
5 - 7 Marshalsea Road
London SE1 1EP
Tel: 0171 828 6266

(NFCA) Scotland

(NFCA) Scotland
1 Melrose Street
Queens Crescent
Glasgow G4 9BJ
Tel: 0141 332 6655

Other organisations

ISSUE

ISSUE is the national self-help organisation which provides information, support and representation to people with fertility difficulties and those who work with them.

Membership   £30 for first year
               then £20 per annum,
               £7.50 low income

ISSUE
114 Lichfield Street
Walsall WS1 1SZ
Tel: 01922 722888

The National Organisation for Counselling Adoptees and their Parents (NORCAP)

NORCAP is a self-help support group for all parties to adoption. It helps adult adopted people to get in touch with their birth parents, as well as offering help and support to birth parents, adoptive parents, and siblings of adopted people. NORCAP maintains a successful Contact Register and publishes a regular newsletter three times a year.

Annual subscription £25.00 including registration (first year); registration £5.00, membership renewal £15.00

Members receive a newsletter three times per year and can buy other publications.

NORCAP
112 Church Road
Wheatley
Oxon OX33 1LU
Tel: 01865 875000

Overseas Adoption Helpline

The **Overseas Adoption Helpline** offers advice and information about current policy and practice in relation to overseas adoption and the legal requirements of the UK and sending countries.

Overseas Adoption Helpline
PO Box 13899
London N6 4WB
Tel: 0990 168742

Useful books and leaflets

| Books for adults

Talking about adoption to your adopted child
PRUE CHENNELLS AND MARJORIE MORRISON
A guide to the whys, whens, and hows of telling adopted children about their origins.
BAAF 1998

Adopters on Adoption:
Reflections on Parenthood and children
DAVID HOWE
This absorbing collection of personal stories of adoptive parents covers topics including assessment and preparation, feelings towards birth mothers and biology, infertility and parenting secure children.
BAAF 1996

Whatever happened to Adam? Stories about disabled children who were adopted or fostered
HEDI ARGENT
This remarkable book tells the stories of 20 young people with disabilities and the families who chose to care for them. All the "children" are now more than 20 years old and *Whatever happened to Adam?* follows their life journeys from joining their families, through childhood and adolescence and into preparation for adulthood.
BAAF 1998

Books for use with children

Chester and Daisy move on
ANGELA LIDSTER
A picture book for 4 - 10-year-olds which tells the story of
two bear cubs that have to leave their family. Work pages are
provided to help children parallel or contrast their own
experiences and feelings.
BAAF 1995

Bruce's Multimedia Story
Bruce is a "spaniel sort of dog" who has to leave his mum and
dad, stay in kennels with his brothers and sisters, and
eventually go to live with a new family.

This computer version of *Bruce's Story* is designed to capitalise
on children's natural interest in computer-based activities and
introduces animation, sound effects, music, speech and
interactivity. The aim is to make the whole experience more
interesting and more fun for the children and hence, more
productive for worker and child together. Information Plus
1998.

Children's book series
A new and unique series of books for use with children
separated from their birth parents. The stories are simply told
and attractively illustrated in full colour. Worksheets at the
back of each book will help children to compare and contrast
their own experiences with those of the characters in the story.
BAAF 1997, 1998

Living with a new family: Nadia and Rashid's story
Nadia is ten and Rashid seven. When their father died some
years ago, their birth mother, Pat, found it hard to look after
them. So Nadia and Rashid went to live with Jenny, a foster
carer, and then with their new parents, Ayesha and Azeez.

Belonging doesn't mean forgetting: Nathan's story
Nathan is a four-year old African-Caribbean boy and has just started school. His birth mum, Rose, found it hard to be a good mum and wanted someone else to look after him. Nathan went to live with foster carers Tom and Delores. And then with Marlene, her daughter Sophie, Grannie and Aunty Bea.

Hoping for the best: Jack's story
Jack is an eight-year-old white boy. His birth mum, Maria, couldn't look after him because she was unhappy and unwell. Jack went to live with Peter and Sarah. At first he was happy but then started to feel sad and mixed up. Peter and Sarah did not think they could be the right mum and dad for him and Jack had to leave.

Feeling Safe: Tina's story – to be published September 1998
Tina wasn't safe at home and now lives with Molly who is her foster carer. Tina had to move after she told a teacher about how her Dad's touches made her feel bad. She is not sure whether she will ever be able to live with her family again but feels safe with her foster family.

Jo's story – to be published September 1998
Tomorrow will be a big day for eight-year-old Joanne. She is going to court with her mum, stepfather and baby brother to be adopted. Jo knows that although Dave isn't her birth father he wants to help look after her for the rest of her life.

Periodicals listing children who need new families

Be My Parent
A national bimonthly newspaper for adopters and permanent foster carers who may or may not be approved. It contains features on adoption and fostering and profiles of children

across the UK who need new permanent families. Subscription details available from BAAF.

Focus on Fives
Focus on Fives is Be My Parent's fortnightly newsletter, featuring children of five and under. It is available on subscription to approved adopters and long-term foster carers.

Children in Scotland
As part of the Scottish Resource Network BAAF's Scottish Centre produces a bimonthly newsletter of children awaiting placement in Scotland. This is distributed to local authorities and voluntary adoption agencies and is available to approved adopters and long-term foster carers.

Adoption UK
Adoption UK is a quarterly journal published by PPIAS and is available on subscription. It keeps members in touch with one another, profiles children needing new permanent families, and gives information on general developments in the field of adoption.

| Advice Notes

BAAF's popular leaflet series called Advice Notes contains essential information about key areas in adoption and fostering.

Adoption - some questions answered
Basic information about adoption. Explains the adoption process including the legal issues and the rights of birth parents.

Foster care - some questions answered
Basic information about fostering. Explains different types of foster care, the relationship with the local authority and legal aspects.

Meeting children's needs through adoption and fostering
Information for people considering adopting or fostering a child
with special needs.

Private Fostering
Aimed at those considering private fostering in England and
Wales, this leaflet explains what private fostering involves, and
provides guidance of what prospective carers need to know.

Stepchildren and adoption
Information for birth parents and step-parents on stepfamilies,
the advantages or not of adoption, and obtaining further advice.

Other useful leaflets

Understanding the assessment process:
Information for prospective adopters and carers
This is a very useful leaflet for anyone thinking about applying
to offer a permanent home to a child. It gives a broad overview
of what will be involved including references, social work
interviews, reports and decision making.

Intercountry adoption – Information and Guidance
Information on adopting a child from overseas, including
procedures, legislation, and where to obtain advice and further
information.

Form ICA
Intercountry adoption form (medical report and development
assessment of child) which, when ordered individually, comes
with two copies of Form Adult 1 for the prospective adoptive
parents.

| **For more information**

For details of current publications and prices contact the
Publications Department at the address below.

☐ Please send me your publications catalogue

☐ Please send me details about *Be My Parent*

☐ Please send me details about BAAF*Link*

☐ Please send me details of how to become an individual
member of BAAF

Send this form to:
Publications Department
BAAF, Skyline House
200 Union Street
London SE1 0LX
Tel: 0171 593 2072

Name

Address

Date

Glossary of terms

Below is a glossary of certain terms that appear in the book. In cases where there is a difference between England and Wales and Scotland, this is shown.

Accommodated/ Accommodation

England and Wales
Under Section 20 of the Children Act 1989 the local authority is required to "provide accommodation" for children "in need" in certain circumstances. The local authority does not acquire parental responsibility (see below) merely by accommodating a child and the arrangements for the child must normally be agreed with the parent(s), who, subject to certain circumstances, are entitled to remove the children from local authority accommodation at any time.

Scotland
Under Section 25 of the Children (Scotland) Act 1995, the local authority must "provide accommodation" for the children in certain circumstances and may also do so in other situations. Normally, the accommodation is provided by agreement with the parent(s), they can then remove the child at any time in most circumstances. Parental responsibilities stay with the parent(s). A child accommodated under section 25 is a "looked after child" (see below).

Adoption Allowance

Adoption agencies (local authority or voluntary adoption societies) can, in certain circumstances, pay a regular allowance to enable an adoption to go ahead which could not otherwise do so for financial reasons. In England and Wales the allowance must be agreed by the agency before the adoption is made.

| Adoption panel

Adoption Agencies (local authorities or voluntary adoption societies) are required to set up an adoption panel which must consider and make recommendations on all children for whom adoption is the plan, and on all matches between prospective adopters and children.

| Contact/Contact Order

England and Wales

Contact may be used to mean visits, including residential visits or other form of direct face-to-face contact between a child and another individual, or it may mean indirect ways of keeping in touch (e.g. letters or telephone calls including letters sent via a third party). A Contact Order under the Children Act is an order requiring the person with whom the child lives to permit the child to have contact (direct or indirect) with the person named in the order.

Scotland

As in England and Wales, contact can mean direct or indirect contact or access. It covers private arrangements (eg. in divorce, etc), it also covers a public law situation when a child is "looked after" by a local authority. When a child is on a supervision requirement (see below) under the children's hearing system, the hearing regulates contact.

| Curator *ad litem*

Similar to Guardian *ad litem* in England and Wales (see below).

| Freeing Order/freeing for Adoption

England and Wales

A Freeing Order under the Adoption Act 1976 ends parents' parental responsibility and transfers parental responsibility to the adoption agency. The purpose of this is to allow any issue regarding parental consent to adoption to be resolved before the child is placed with prospective adopters. In certain circumstances the 'former parent' may ask the court to revoke the order if the child is not placed with prospective adopters after one year.

Scotland

A Freeing Order under the Adoption (Scotland) Act 1978 has the same effect as above. It is an optional court process by a local authority before an application for adoption.

| Fostering/foster care

In this book this term is used for those cases where a child is placed with a foster carer approved by the local authority and/or placed directly by a voluntary organisation. These placements are governed by the Foster Placement (Children) Regulations 1991 in England and Wales and by the Fostering of Children (Scotland) Regulations 1996 in Scotland. "Short-term", "long-term" and "permanent" foster care and "respite care" may mean different things to different people – they are not legally defined terms.

| Guardian

A guardian is a person who has been formally appointed as a child's guardian after the death of one or both parents. The appointment may be made in writing by a parent or by a court.

| Guardian *ad litem*

England and Wales

A person appointed by the court to safeguard a child's interests in court proceedings. Local authorities are required to establish panels of people to act as guardians *ad litem* (and reporting officers – see below) in care proceedings and in adoption proceedings. Their duties are set out in court rules and include presenting a report to the court.

| In care

Applies only to England and Wales. A child who is subject to a Care Order is described as being "in care". A Care Order gives the local authority parental responsibility for the child but does not deprive the parent(s) of this. Nevertheless, the local authority may limit the extent to which parents may exercise their parental responsibility and may override parental wishes in the interests of the child's welfare.

| Looked after

England and Wales
This term includes both children "in care" and accommodated children. Local authorities have certain duties towards all looked after children and their parents, which are set out in the Children Act 1989. These include the duty to safeguard and promote the child's welfare and the duty to consult with children and parents before taking decisions.

Scotland
This term covers all children for whom the local authority has responsibilities under section 17 the Children (Scotland) Act 1995. It replaces the term "in care". It is wider than and different from the English and Welsh definition. It includes children at home as well as those placed away from home.

| Open adoption

This term may be used very loosely and can mean anything from an adoption where a child continues to have frequent face-to-face contact with members of his or her birth family to an adoption where there is some degree of "openness", eg. the birth family and adopters meeting each other once. People using the term should be asked to define what they mean!

| Parental responsibility

England and Wales
This is defined in the Children Act 1989 as 'all the rights, duties, powers and responsibilities which by law a parent has in relation to a child and his property'. When a child is born to married parents they will both share parental responsibility for him or her, and this parental responsibility can never be lost except on the making of an

Adoption Order. A father who is not married to the child's mother does not automatically have parental responsibility but may acquire it either by formal agreement with the mother or by court order. Confusingly the term "parents" when used in the Children Act includes both parents, whether or not the father has parental responsibility, but in the Adoption Act 1976, "parent" means only parents who have parental responsibility.

Parental Responsibilities and Rights – Scotland

These are what parents have for their children and are defined in sections 1 and 2 of the Children (Scotland) Act 1995. All mothers have them automatically; fathers only if married to the mother at conception or later. However, fathers can get them by formal agreement with the mother or by a court order.

Anyone can go to court for an order about parental responsibilities and rights under section 11 of the Children (Scotland) Act 1995. Residence orders (see below) and contact orders (see above) are examples. The court can also take away responsibilities and rights under this section.

Parents or others with responsibilities and rights can only lose them by a court order: an Adoption Order; Parental Responsibilities Order (see below); or an order under section 11.

In relation to a father who is not married to the mother, in Scotland, the father can obtain these rights through an agreement under the Children (Scotland) Act 1995.

Parental Responsibilities Order

Scotland

This section removes all parental responsibility from the parent(s) (except the right to consent (or not) to adoption) and gives them to the local authority. It is granted under section 86 of the Children (Scotland) Act 1995.

| Reporting officer

A member of the panel of guardians *ad litem*/curators *ad litem* and reporting officers, appointed by the court for adoption proceedings. His or her specific task is to ensure that the agreement of a parent or guardian to an Adoption Order if given is given freely and with full understanding of what is involved and to witness the agreement.

| Residence order

England and Wales
An order under the Children Act 1989 settling the arrangements as to the person/s with whom the child is to live. Where a Residence Order is made in favour of someone who does not already have parental responsibility for the child (eg. a relative or foster carer) that person will acquire parental responsibilities subject to certain restrictions (eg. they will not be able to consent to the child's adoption). Parental responsibility given in connection with a Residence Order will only last as long as the Residence Order. A Residence Order normally only lasts until the child's 16th birthday.

Scotland
This is one of the orders possible under section 11 of the Children (Scotland) Act 1995. It regulates with whom the child lives. If the person with the Residence Order did not have any parental responsibilities and rights before, the order gives those as well.

| Residence order allowance

England and Wales
Local authorities have a power to contribute to the cost of a child's maintenance when the child is living with somebody under a Residence Order provided he or she is not living with a parent or step-parent. A financial contribution under this power is normally referred to as a Residence Order allowance.

Scotland
Local authorities have the power to pay an allowance to a person who has care of a child and who is not a parent or a foster carer. The person does not have to have a Residence Order.

Schedule 2 report

England and Wales
Under the court rules for adoption proceedings, a report has to be submitted to the court covering the details that are set out in Schedule 2 to the Adoption Rules 1984. In the case of an adoption which has been arranged by an adoption agency, or an application to free a child for adoption, this report is the responsibility of the placement agency. In cases where the adoption was not arranged by an adoption agency (eg, step-parents or intercountry adoption) the local authority prepares the report.

Section 23 or Section 22 reports

Scotland
Reports to the court are under section 23 in agency adoptions and section 22 in non-agency cases eg. step-parents of the Adoption (Scotland) Act 1978. The Rules of Court give guidance about what should be in the reports.

Supervision requirements

Scotland
These are the orders made by the children's hearing for any child needing compulsory measures of supervision. Children may be victims of abuse or neglect, have other problems and/or have committed crimes. All children on supervision requirements are "looked after" by the local authority, even if they live at home. Supervision requirements do not give parental responsibilities and rights to local authorities.